How to Make Friends

A Step-By-Step Guide to Meeting People and Building Relationships

Jess Riley

Table of Contents

Introduction:
Initiating the Journey

We cannot live only for ourselves. A thousand fibers connect us with our fellow men; and among those fibers, as sympathetic threads, our actions run as causes, and they come back to us as effects. –Herman Melville

Most people know they need to connect with other people. Even those who do not feel that way also know they have to depend upon some sort of connection with others. A lot of people who call themselves "introverts" lie somewhere on a spectrum between craving a bond with another person and wanting personal space. The good thing? We can have both. Sometimes we just need the right support from the right people.

So, why are we reluctant to bond with others? What makes us halt in our steps? What stops us from smiling more and sharing deeper details about our lives? The answers to these questions can be subjective. Some people are shy. It is as simple as that. They would like to connect with others, yet they fail to initiate this connection. They may tag along with a group to parties, meet you for a date, or accompany you to a concert or a doctor's appointment, but they would still be shy. This is different from *introversion*, when opening up is both difficult and unfavorable; such people tend to focus inward rather than outward. This is also different from having trust issues, fears, or social anxiety. Trusting anyone, from a total stranger to an acquaintance or even a family member, can take time. Some people may have deep-seated fears of being judged or made fun of. Others may be socially anxious due to their poor mental health or low self-esteem. These sorts of people may struggle to connect with others, and they need an extra push to not only feel better but also connect better.

Why I Wrote This Book

Want to say "hello" to someone without feeling lost on what to do about the long awkward pause that follows? Wish to talk to your sweet neighbor who smiles at you every morning as you leave for work, but don't know how to introduce yourself? Long to ask a colleague out for coffee, yet want to avoid looking like a total creep? Well, you have found yourself the right book that explains why you are unable to go ahead and just be normal in front of people. But hold on—this book explains the hurdles in addition to telling you how you can cross these hurdles. And why shouldn't we cross these hurdles if we want to live better lives? We look around and see people are happy with their tribe, but choosing a tribe is a risk not many of us are ready to take. So, instead, we convince ourselves that we are better off alone. Although, deep down, we know being alone is not very helpful.

Being alone may not be tiring for people, but feeling lonely is; these are two very different things. While people may choose to be alone because they prefer it, no one chooses to be lonely. You cannot be best friends with someone if you have just met them. You would want to know them first. Similarly, you have to open up to help them get to know you as well. Most people prefer a midpoint where they don't need best friends, but they don't want isolation either. Yet, even to have good friends in life, we have to have the courage to open up to some extent. Opening up might seem like a Herculean task when small talk is the first hurdle. So many of us find the thought of initiating a conversation deeply troubling. It makes us anxious and overwhelmed.

In this book, my efforts are toward breaking this massive task down into many smaller tasks that can help readers understand the psyche behind these troubles and how they can overcome them to approach anyone and everyone. I understand why making friends is important, but I also understand why it is tough, and this is the very reason I am inspired to write this book. To make friends easily, we need to first befriend ourselves. When we know ourselves better, we understand who we want to be friends with and why. With this understanding, we can begin to ease and empower ourselves with tools that can help us navigate through tough situations.

What Is in It for the Readers?

Aloofness can be comforting. However, it is in those slow, steady moments when life takes a backseat and loneliness creeps in that we are reminded of how we are missing something wonderful: the company of wonderful people, joy, laughter, and greater fulfillment in life.

This book can help readers to discover meaningful ways to talk to people. Talking to others can be emotionally challenging, but when we harness some of the following practical tips, we then can readily approach a stranger, initiate a small talk with them, and end up having a long conversation. Not all meetings can lead to fruitful friendships, but if we are lucky enough to meet someone who shares our values, then it's possible to nurture a lifelong friendship. Of course, many other factors matter, timing being a crucial one. However, the myth that you have to change yourself to be likable must be busted. There is nothing wrong with being shy. Shyness can be a charming aspect of one's personality. You can be friendly and still be private regarding details about your life. It is not possible, nor wise, to open up the first time you meet a stranger. The problem occurs when this shyness limits us and our possibilities.

Overcoming your shyness is not altering your personality. It is just readily learning the social skills that can help you come up with quick lines about the weather, food, pop culture, politics, fashion, and even dad jokes.

Whether or not your friendship will stand the test of time is only for time to tell, but as long as you are ready to be friends with others, you should be good. This book is well researched when it comes to strategies that work best to gain friends. It doesn't matter if you're a student, parent, working professional, young adult, or an alien who has stepped into a new world; if you want to explore friendships, you have picked up the right book. Through a variety of examples, this book provides suggestions for reflecting on different kinds of situations. It explains why we may feel some friends are truer than others, what makes them more reliable, and how we can put in the right effort to keep such friends forever. This book can help you stay relevant today and tomorrow.

About Me

I am Jess Riley, and I am a seasoned professional turned author. My origins are from Scotland, but I made the epic move to New Zealand, where I am now settled with my family.

My passion to help others form meaningful connections comes from what I have personally experienced with loneliness and social isolation. Growing up, I was always the shy and quiet one who struggled to make friends. Making friends was an achievement, and I can gladly say I've earned some great friends in this life. But I know it was not easy, and it still isn't. People presume that shy people like us don't like to talk much, falsely interpreting our actions as disinterest. While our behavior may portray disinterest, shy people crave social connection as much as bold and confident people.

My previous career meant I had to move around a lot, and, as a result, I faced the added challenge of having to constantly adapt to new environments and make new friends. My experience has taught me to not only cope with but also counter these struggles.

Through research, resource gathering, self-improvement, and personal growth, my journey to overcoming my social anxiety and building lasting friendships motivated me to start writing. With an aim to inspire and empower others to embark on their own journey toward success, I present to you this book—a labor of love, pain, practical experience, passion, power, earnestness, and hard work.

Chapter 1:
The Importance of Building Social Connections

Lucky are those people who have someone to brighten their day. Be it a boring lecture or the same mundane office, if you have the right friend at the right place, meeting you at the right time, you know your day is saved. You know you have someone who can both lend an ear and inspire you.

Take the story of Michelle. After she lost her husband, John, she felt really lonely. While it was the same place she had grown up, it seemed alien to her now. Not that she did not have any friends—she had several in her hometown—but she was very unwelcoming to everyone around her, including family. She did not feel like going out anymore or meeting anyone. Everything seemed pointless now. Apart from that, she had her 2-year-old daughter, Suzie, to take care of. Life was like a blurry image passing her by, a massive poster of happy faces, and she tried to find her own, but she knew no one in that image. Who were these people who looked so happy? Was life deliberately harsh on her and her little girl? She used to keep asking herself the same questions again and again. Then, one day, there came next-door Sylvia, a 62-year-old woman who had served in the navy all her life—single, and yet to be fulfilled. One evening, Sylvia visited Michelle. In her hand was a tray covered with an embroidered cloth. It smelled like freshly baked banana bread, and while Michelle was not very keen on meeting anyone that evening, for some odd reason, she could not resist this energy. As they say, "love thy neighbor." Ever since that day, their now decade-long bond has been growing stronger. These two women had nothing in common. Their friendship demonstrates that just one evening, one honest conversation, and one bond of trust can change our lives. The evening the two had met, Michelle cried like a baby. Not that she had not been weeping all these days, but there was something about crying in front of a stranger who did not seem like a stranger anymore. Sylvia had told Michelle about Jim, her partner she had lost to cancer. She shared about numerous friends she had lost over the years and what it had taught her.

In this world, affection is easier to find than honest friendships. Michelle did not need pity; she wanted to feel validated. Most people who had met her were asking her to move on. Everyone reminded her that it had been four months and that she really needed to turn the page, and now all the more because she had to take care of Suzie. She had to find a way to start working again to not just be financially secure but also to find a distraction. But, sometimes, we want to face our grief rather than suppress it with distractions. Sylvia was the first one to hold Michelle's hand and say it was okay to cry and not want to move on. There are times when we want to feel human enough to just be, and true friends are those who just let us be.

Do We Need to Socialize to Make Friends?

Not necessarily. Michelle was lucky that Sylvia approached her. Most of us crave some sort of social connection but are too afraid to make a move. There is a fear of rejection, but more so, we succeed in convincing ourselves that we're fine the way we are. We have all sorts of explanations ready in our heads to avoid any social interaction. But, sometimes, we do need to go out to meet people. Not all of us are confident enough to leave our comfort zone to go meet a new person, but then it becomes a matter of missed opportunities and no effort, only regrets.

Friends Can Make Us Happier and Healthier

There are many heartwarming stories of true friendship, some we know about while most we do not. Friends make us happier because they are the people who we can bother at any given time. These are the people who we know we can trust, who have got our back, and who are the happiest when we achieve something. People do not build friendships anticipating the benefits that will come along. This is why true friendships cannot be measured in terms of give-and-take. Just as we cannot measure joy, we cannot compare the sources of joy. Today, you and your friend can be elated because your favorite team won the match. Tomorrow, you both can celebrate graduating together, and, some years down the lane, you both will be a part of each other's weddings. What you both can be certain about is creating memories. Yet, comparing memories is unfair, because, in platonic relationships, two people constantly strive to form a meaningful bond. When two people bond over enriching each other's lives, there is no competition or jealousy.

The absence of negative feelings and contributions to each other's lives is proof enough of why people seek genuine friendships. Positive feelings are contagious, and so is joy. Not all group settings are positive; some can harbor toxicity. But people like to take this risk and socialize only in the hopes of finding true friendships. Not all people who readily socialize meet other good people, but their chances of making friends are still higher than it is for those who are sitting alone in their house binge-watching shows on an over-the-top platform. If you visit a place on vacation, you will remember its people for their warmth, friendliness, and hospitality as much as you'll remember the place for its beauty, food, and charm. This is because human connections can leave a lasting impression on mental, emotional, and physical health. People tend to be attracted to those who are positive, helpful, and kind. Their conduct can make us happy and leave a good impression. It is their energy that is contagious, and we instantly know that we want to be friends with them.

Energy That Is Contagious

Negative feelings and behavior are also contagious, which is probably why people prefer to steer clear of such negativity. Imagine having a road rage incident; it's possible that we come back home and the spillover effect influences our family. But, at the same time, a person feeling sad may instantly feel better in the company of good friends. This is because happy and positive emotions can no doubt improve our individual and collective experiences. While sadness gets dim in the collective, it has deliberative and intense effects on people in isolation. The spillover of positive feelings happens in positive settings when we are surrounded by people who make us happy. There is no small talk between friends, as you both can converse for hours. It can be mindless chatting about something or an essential discussion regarding something important. Even if you do not meet them every day, you are not worried about not being on the same page. You know things between you two will not change, and there is always a scope to catch up. This assurance that we get from friends is very helpful to be happy. It is a huge reliability factor. We know we have someone to talk to, who can listen to us without judgment, who we can ask for help, and who would be honest with us no matter what.

It is our friends who we turn to when there is a problem—not just an external problem but also internal stress. After all, apart from our families, it's our friends who make up our social support system. This is a major stress relief factor. Genuine and dependable friendships can also improve mental well-being (Mental Health First Aid USA, 2019). With a greater sense of purpose and meaning in life, we have more balance, too. We become less dependent on negative coping methods like smoking, drinking, doing drugs, and bearing all the burden in isolation. This also ensures better memories and improved cognitive functions.

While stress can inflame the arteries, a stronger and healthier response to stress can have a positive cardiovascular effect (Johns Hopkins Medicine, n.d.). Poor social support does not give a protective layer around mental and physical health. A good social support system also helps us cope with trauma better. This is because when we are scared or tense, we're thrown into fight-or-flight mode, which can induce the synthesis and release of cortisol. This situation is exacerbated when we feel we're stuck in an adverse situation alone. When we have people around us, we do not dramatically shift into an extremely defensive mode. Chronic stress may also cause immunosuppression, hyperactivity, hormone imbalance, and hypertension (Santos-Longhurst, 2018). To avoid all this, we need a stress-resilience plan, and social support increases stress resilience by enhancing the ability to optimize the neurochemical stress response.

What Does Social Support Mean?

People who are accessible to you through social ties are your *social support*. They can be individuals, groups, communities, your therapist, neighbor, friends, or family. These are the people who are around when you need psychological, emotional, physical, or financial help. The size of this network does not matter. Sometimes how often you interact with them does not matter either. Interaction with people who support you is instrumental because it gives balance to how you function as an entity. How the support develops depends both on the supporter and the one being supported.

For example, any trauma from childhood that carries itself into a person's adulthood is a defining factor in shaping their personality. Rich social networks do not have to be powerful connections; these have to be fulfilling relations where equals participate. People in such groups don't engage in risky behavior or harbor collective negative emotions. Your social support group is one that cultivates healthy treatment of all members and positive coping mechanisms.

Sometimes, wonderful things happen, and maybe we should just let them happen to us. Rue, aged 26, used to work at the public defender's office while also working part-time at a store to support her income and pay off her student debt. This meant she was so tired on some days and nights that she didn't have enough motivation and energy to cook meals. It was during these 3 years that Megan from work was her savior, friend, and confidant. On some days, Megan would bring food from home and leave it for Rue without saying a word; that was 7 years ago. You do not have to have a to-do list with your friends. You don't even have to always express what you feel. Some friends are a blessing, and they understand. They go out of their way to make sure they bring some joy and ease to your life. Rue and Megan may not be working at the same place anymore. They may not have much engagement either. In fact, liking each other's pictures on social media is the most interaction they have these days now, but Megan was, undoubtedly, a part of Rue's social support system back in the day.

Friendships do not have to include unusual demands, long conversations, never-ending chats with smileys; some friendships survive without the obvious. They can simply include the understanding that when you turn to the people you love, you would not be disappointed. Remembering the past can sometimes move you to tears and other times make you burst out laughing. But, one thing is for sure: Life is never dull with the ones you love. Your support system, thus, gives you a channel to be emotionally expressive. You have the courage to be your true self in front of them. All the scattered pieces of your brain suddenly pick themselves up and become intact, even if temporarily, when a friend brings you your comfort food. Everything is suddenly okay when your friend helps you find that important document you've lost. It all seems normal when one hug solves all of life's mysterious problems. Stronger relationships breed a stronger support system which makes you feel strong and resilient against troubles, diseases, tensions, and unpleasant surprises.

Prioritizing Socialization: Understanding the Science of Friendships

Prioritizing socialization is necessary for overall well-being. But what about people who are shy? Moving to a new city for college was very difficult for Rex. He had never lived away from home. His place was a single room, so he had no roommates, something that he was both thankful for and sad about. When you have no say as to who you live with, you may not always be pleased with the results. At the same time, having no one around can be quite depressing, too. Eventually, this shy guy of 17 looked for ways to meet new people, as well as develop new ways to interact by cultivating newer interests. Now, he's part of his college's photography club and has a chance to meet new people every weekend.

Some people go out of their way to socialize because their loneliness begins to overpower them. The obstacles in our way while attempting to socialize become our reasons to socialize even more. These hindrances are not all behavioral in nature. Some other hindrances could be a result of a lack of time, not enough opportunities, routine, culture, fear of commitment, and irrational worries. It is interesting to note that these causes become our incentive to go out and meet new people, otherwise we have bigger fears on a daily basis, like

- Why can't I connect with other people?
- Is there a problem with me?
- What if I remain alone?
- I don't have any friends.
- I don't have a life.

These fears eventually lead us to one ultimate question: *What should I do to make friends?*

All About Social Connections

Social connections not only help us to feel less isolated, but they also improve our sense of self-worth and add to our sense of well-being. It helps the mind and body be balanced. However, it is the fine art of getting along where most people fail. Socializing is not just about meeting and smiling or talking about similar interests. It's also about building real connections in the real world. It does not matter whether you are a homemaker or an engineer. Socializing is an art, and it sells. We have to package ourselves in a way that we're able to convey what's in our best interest, without coming off as rude, and then connect with those who have similar interests or knowledge about our fields of interest. This also means we have to make connections with people who can help and encourage us to be our better selves. But why would someone want to be our friend unless we have something to offer to them as well? What would be our charm? Are our hobbies interesting enough? Are our interests worthy enough? Are our ambitions big enough? Are our problems problematic enough? Instead of obsessing about these questions—which we do mostly in our spare time—our focus must be on going out and finding the answers for ourselves.

Socialization may or may not have positive impacts, but one thing is for sure, and that is that socialization provides us more opportunities than we would get sitting isolated in our rooms. Positive opportunities protect us, whereas negative ones make us more vulnerable. The ones with beneficial effects may allow personal growth, help us sort our careers, propel positive connections, and even improve our mental, physical, and emotional health. Through socialization, we have a better understanding of others and of ourselves.

You could be shy and not a people pleaser, love being alone, or enjoy the company of your pet more than other people, yet socializing of some form can help you lead a better life. Humans are social animals, and, most times, we prefer living in a community. We may not have a direct engagement with people around us, but we are indirectly dependent. From someone who delivers your food to going to a police station to lodge a complaint, in the extremes of life situations and in all situations floating between these two extreme points, you have to interact with the people around you. Humans tend to function better due to this dependency.

If you are someone who has minimal interactions with people, you can start with interacting with those who you have most interaction with. It could be a cashier, a waiter, a delivery person, or even someone online. Maintaining a conversation is tougher than initiating a conversation, and this is where social skills come into play. We must remember that socialization

- is a long and an ever-evolving process.
- happens in all stages of life.
- identifies and expects some basic values and principles in a particular social setup.
- enables a person to enact certain roles in society and also perform some duties.
- discourages negative behavior toward other people.

Socialization can be *primary*, when one follows the norms of the house and family. It can also be *secondary*, when norms, behavior, and values are absorbed from the surroundings outside of the family. These could occur in schools, colleges, playgrounds, churches, offices, public places, or even tourist spots. Realistically, the process of socialization, primary or secondary, never ends. It keeps involving and evolving the person on the journey.

Let us see some of the reasons why we need to socialize and how to be better at it.

Socializing for Personality Development

We begin socializing from birth, and this also becomes a factor in shaping our personality. Kids who grow up in a friendlier, happier, and safer atmosphere tend to have a personality that is kinder, more open, loving, respectful, flexible, tolerant, secure, and approachable. Socialization is an important factor in developing our minds, bodies, attitudes, emotions, behaviors, and, thus, the interactions we have as children with our environment. This social group has a point of view on things, and these children are conditioned to think beyond the "self." Such people, when grown, do not have a problem when they have to seek help. They are not shamed for things they fail at or do not understand. This can make them more resilient and fearless. Kids who grow up alone tend to get more nervous in a crowd. They grow up to be adults who may feel socially handicapped or awkward. Their personality tends to be someone who looks at self-interests only and escapes public scenarios as soon as possible (Ng, 2021). Not liking people is not necessarily a bad thing, but not being able to survive among people can be frustrating, exhausting, and self-defeating.

Socializing for a Sharper Mind

With the regulation of human behavior in social settings, there is more focus on work that needs to be done. Not only are signs and gestures a good way to train the mind, but language, vocabulary, grammar, and elocution add to brain function (Jiang, 2018). Being able to converse is both an art and a skill, and this improves the cognitive side of the brain. Networking keeps our minds active and agile. While growing up, a child participates in different activities like debates, drama, dance, or speeches, all of which prepare them for an audience. When taking part in group activities like science projects or adventure sports, they are introduced to teamwork and team building. All these activities exercise and challenge the brain and improve cognitive function. Because it strengthens our connection to our present, past, and future, social interactions are a strong component of strengthening our memory, too.

Socializing for Better Connections

There are certain rules when one is socializing with the aim of forming better connections. One is expected to regulate their emotions when trying to connect to people with power, prestige, and position. It comes with controlling emotions to gain confidence, support, and social approval. This kind of socialization is usually for better opportunities. The more we interact with people, the more we understand the purpose and motive behind the agenda of these social agents. The more we understand this behavior, the better we place ourselves in this social world and how to further our interests through deliberation, analysis, observation, interaction, detection, and interpretation.

Socializing to Develop New Skills and Interests

Socialization is an opportunity to learn new things. It is our window to get introduced to things that others are practicing. No theoretical knowledge is enough unless a person has adequate practical knowledge, and to gain practical knowledge, one has to engage in fieldwork. Social behavior is a part of social learning, which in turn is a part of social capital. What you may feel is useless office chitchat can actually help improve your workplace relationships. This can make collaboration effective and efficient. While "socializing" may sound like a big bogus word, only people with true social skills would know how to employ them to become more productive. Forming a common social identity and being inclusive with your norms; believing in social growth and having social support of all around you; earning social fabric by strengthening the fabric of trust and reliability; and, finally, being present at the right time at the right place can help not just socialize but lead the process in a social setting.

Socializing for Better Health

Healthier people attract more friends because we all are naturally attracted to something or someone that has a positive effect on others. Healthier people are also those who complain less and focus on living a fuller life. This is also a cycle: Health supports better socialization skills, and better socialization skills encourage good health. On the other hand, competition, bitterness, narrow-mindedness, and hostility perpetuate behaviors more focused on the self rather than others. Such people can never have good social skills, let alone leadership skills. Healthier and more successful people lead one another toward progress. This is what most people seek in social connections: mutual benefit.

While isolation has been wrongly associated with depression and early death, isolation does have negative effects on the mind, body, and souls of most people. Yes, isolation can bring peace and stability to some, but, in many cases, isolation is a forced condition rather than a choice. Social isolation is considered to be a cause of dementia. About 50% of dementia risks increase due to social isolation, while poor social relationships are believed to increase the risk of heart disease by 29% and risks of stroke by 32%. Loneliness also pushes forward anxiety and suicidal thoughts. People who feel socially isolated generally see themselves as different from others or as outcasts (Centers for Disease Control and Prevention, 2022).

Socialization, on the other hand, where living beings are considered social beings, thrives in a culture of togetherness. These values are passed down from one generation to the next. Interestingly, most people today would agree that they are less social than their parents.

From the Author's Life

Loneliness is something that we all face at some stage in our lives. I remember one period of my life when I felt genuinely lonely. Loneliness was never an issue for me before that, as I quite enjoyed my own company. I always had a lot to do, and because I was quiet and shy, I preferred peace. Being shy was not a problem because I did not feel I needed help when it came to making friends. I was cordial, approachable, and easy to talk to. I had friends and family to support me, which made my life complete. However, this one time, I had a job opportunity, and I availed it. I was working with a group of people that was selected for a 24-month-long project for which I had to move to another city. All the other members of the team were local to the area, and I was the only "outsider." Work was normal. In fact, I enjoyed working there. My colleagues were nice, and I had a nice working relationship with all of them. Although I developed meaningful friendships with my colleagues at work, our social interactions remained confined to a professional setting. Because they were all locals, they could plan every evening with their friends and family after work. Meanwhile, my temporary presence meant I had no social life outside of work.

On most evenings, I was on my own. If you are someone who prefers solitude, you may feel this is a perfect setting. However, most people who love solitude know the difference between being lonely and being alone. In my case, I was both alone and lonely. I was fine at first and could manage these evenings to some extent, but then they became a norm.

This went on for several months, and when things did not seem to be improving, I started to weigh my options. I had to because the circumstances were affecting me. It feels different when you know you have a support system around you. All the people who cared for me and who I cared for were far away. I finally made the decision to quit the project and move back to my home city.

I know many of you may feel that there are sacrifices we have to make to move ahead in our careers, and I am all for such sacrifices. But sacrifices affect us differently, and this is the reason we end up making different choices in life. For me, at that point in life, preserving myself was more important than a career opportunity. I feel I was lucky because not everyone is privileged enough to make such choices. However, choosing what makes us happy and complete should never be a privilege or a sacrifice; it must be our right.

My life is a different example now. It's been more than ten years since I've been away from my family, and "away" is a small term because I live on the other side of the world now. Do I feel lonely sometimes? Yes. I've struggled with loneliness over all these years, and that is not because I am alone. I absolutely love the life I have with my husband and our own small family of the four-legged variety. I guess it is the people and the life that I have lived that I miss. It was fulfilling in its own way, but so is the life I live now. I do feel the physical absence of my friends and family, but, more than that, I guess I feel the joy that comes from everlasting bonds. When we refer to *social* connections, we mean *everlasting* connections. There is joy in growing old with the people you love because there is no end to knowing them, and it keeps getting better with time.

If I have to tell people about the best way they can live their lives, I would say it is by really cherishing their friends and family. I know work, as well as your alone time, is important, but the time you spend with the people you love never comes back, and it is always falling short. This time is a testament to a life well lived. Everything else, even loneliness, is a relative catchphrase.

Food for Thought

Do you initiate contact with your friends if it has been more than three weeks since you last spoke to them?

An option to consider:

Sometimes we fail to initiate contact because our personal and professional lives can keep us busy. But it is the time of digital media. One good way to keep in touch with old friends and colleagues is by making them feel special from time to time. It is not very demanding because, firstly, once you understand how to use digital and social media as tools, you learn to dominate it. Secondly, you have to do this once in a while. So, you can always post a picture of your friend on their birthday. Birthdays are special no matter what age, and we all want to feel special on this day. If you feel your friend is an introvert, do not make it public, though make sure you send them a personalized message to make them feel special. Ask them what time you should call them, or tell them you would call them over the weekend. This is something you can plan from time to time rather than only on special occasions. Once or twice a month, you two can have a little ritual to keep in touch and keep each other updated.

Chapter 2:
The Evolution of Social Connections

The art of greeting has evolved over the centuries. Maybe a few hundred years ago, I would bring you flowers to impress and befriend you. I can do that in today's world as well, but it would be a sad case if I find that you are allergic to them. Some people are allergic to good manners and etiquette. What you find attractive may come across as very formal to someone else. That does not make either of you wrong or right; it just makes the two of you different. Can you both still be friends? There is a possibility.

Social connections have evolved the way different communities have evolved. Some communities still put others before the individual, while many liberal communities focus on individuals and their rights before thinking of the community as an entity. The smallest entity is a person, but what values we as people prefer varies from place to place. There is no denying, however, the fact that the immediate envelopment surrounding each individual is their family. Lucky are the ones who have had a secure and happy childhood. They are the ones who grow up to be caring and nurturing. The ones who become self-absorbed and paranoid are not negative, but they may be the ones who had to fend for themselves at a younger age. Perhaps they learned ways to protect themselves first and then go out into the world. The walls around them are not high because they disdain human connection but because they prefer reservations over vulnerability.

When looking for friends, we look for people who can understand us and our layers, flaws, problems, and expectations. We look for people who would help us before judging us, advise us before scolding us, and save us before blaming us.

Why Did Humans Become Less Social?

Social ties in older times were formed by living together in groups, sharing whatever resources people had, and helping and protecting each other. Today, we know what boundaries are and when to form them. We're aware of when we need a buffer around ourselves to maintain energy, resilience, and peace. In olden times, peace, power, and prosperity came via the connections one had, which meant that a person who knew influential people then had influence over others. Despite the fact a lot has changed and we live with the reality that friends meet by chance and remain friends by luck, we humans still look for influential, rather than genuine and meaningful, connections. Influence brings, to many of us, purpose and meaning in life; this is one connotation that has not changed a lot. We are willing to compromise when we see benefits. There is always an element of selective advantage when making adjustments, for there are no adjustments made where there are no benefits to be reaped.

Why Is Making Friends So Hard?

One obvious reason is the lack of trust. Most people are afraid of being taken advantage of. We choose the deadliness of loneliness over placing our trust in someone new, and this becomes worse as we grow older. We have changed because our social values have changed. If we go back two generations, people had more time to spend with each other. There was a lot more social interaction through sports, meetings, cultural events, entertainment, and mobilization. People did not come back home to sit in one corner; they went out again to meet friends and chat for long hours. A very significant element of this social value was to help someone in need. People used to come forward to be useful. To serve others was an important purpose in life. When the economic dynamics of the world changed, so did the social values. War was one reason why people became more selfish. They looked inward instead of outward, and why wouldn't they? Most of them had lost everything and had to begin from nothing all over again. They did not have time to help others while they were trying to save themselves. On the other hand, those who fought wars were sent off to distant lands, away from their home and families and everything they knew to go fight. This was a destructive turn in the history of the human species, as humans are meant to be constructive and innovative.

Competition, which was both a cause and consequence of war, made people more self-centered. These were the values we passed on to the next generation as well. Now people wanted to befriend their equals—economic equals. Social fragmentation occurred when children were taught to create a separate identity instead of becoming a part of society. This major shift in human behavior caused an identity crisis, because humans are meant to be social animals and not isolated robots. Competition was a miniaturized version of war in society where people fought for the same limited resources. Social values changed. People were marginalized every day on the basis of race, religion, region, color, and gender, which only kept growing. Because competition is so harsh on most of us, we may be left feeling isolated and incompatible. Making friends, thus, becomes even more difficult. This crisis peaked again during the recent COVID times. And this is the sad truth about human connection: People seek profit before they seek meaningful friendships, and they would rather choose isolation than quit being selective and competitive.

Comparison is an offshoot of competition. We get jealous when we see someone else progressing. Our focus is on someone else's promotion and not on our own performance. And as petty and tiring things are in a world where everything and everyone has a monetary tag, it is a fact that we fear rejections more today because we feel we are not "worth" it. So what do we do to preserve ourselves? We stick to our old friends, and if we have none, we prefer staying that way.

Several other reasons make building friendships particularly difficult in today's age:

- It is difficult to maintain friendships.
- People have expensive tastes, and being on your own is economical and liberating.
- Trust issues hold people back from being vulnerable.

Some other reasons are

- **Changing nature of work**: Our work keeps us busy, but it also keeps us isolated, tired, and in a toxic retrace.
- **More isolated lives**: With nuclear families, the old community system is broken. Back in the day, people used to sit and talk, and talking was therapy. Talking opened many doors of opportunities just as it resolved conflicts. We do not have honest conversations anymore. Some do not have time, and others are just not interested.
- **Different priorities**: Making friends is a priority only when people have a certain vested interest. This is true for most people, but if you are someone who is looking for genuine friendship, you need to find someone who has a similar intention.
- **Netflix and chill**: This phrase was made for people who isolate, and the phenomenon is, sadly, working because we are getting increasingly chained to this sort of lifestyle.
- **Lost the soul connection**: This is mainly due to how we tag others. People prefer single, isolated lives as it is more convenient, but it works against our psyche. People stay away from others to avoid being disappointed. They feel different opinions and values cannot coexist, yet it is a mistake to think that because that is what makes the world more diverse, beautiful, and cheerful.

Regaining Trust in Social Values and Social Connections

Regaining trust, especially after we feel our trust has been broken, is like taking a leap of faith without knowing what faith is anymore. We need social connections and relationships in life to not just survive but also live a fuller life. In social connections, there are always shared meanings and values, and the noble aim is to pass these on to others and learn from others what we lack. There is also another aspect to socialization, which is to appreciate and learn to receive appreciation. Appreciation is not always grand flattery as it also involves constructive criticism. Such positive support is central to any society's growth. We have to be receptive to both flattery and meaningful suggestions.

Every time we meet someone and move forward to form a new bond, we wish them to fulfill our needs and expectations we have from that equation. These needs and expectations could either be intentional or unintentional, but when we are close to finding a proper match, we feel relieved. We know in our hearts that we have found a reliable and honest person. However, when we are reaching out to someone, being vulnerable, or opening up, we're putting more than our emotions at risk. Some people who easily make friends are ready to take this risk, but others are more protective of their hearts. All risks come with consequences, so we need to accept that we'll never acquire everything that we want. Hence, it is very important to learn to be thankful for mediocrity, for perfection is a myth.

We have to begin with the beginning. Thus, we have to instill these values in ourselves before expecting things from others. We can't look for perfection when looking for a partner. We look for emotions because we want a relationship, not a business deal. Similarly, we have to be realistic when we are looking for friends. A child learns to recognize and respond to the shared meanings and expectations from others only through the process of socialization. I am helping my neighbor because I must, and not with the expectation that they will help me, too. Just as there is no perfect neighbor or partner, there can never be a perfect friend. But can we find perfection in our friend? Yes, we can, and it will depend on how we view perfection.

The norms, and values may differ within a society in different families belonging to different cultures, regions, and strata, but the basic need for a friend remains the same. So, while socialization is necessary, we need to look at our needs and the needs of the other person. If you feel you both can vibe well, you should greet them. And no number of awkward pauses can stop you two from becoming friends.

Social capital is necessary for social well-being and efficiency, not just for higher pay. There are certain benefits to being social or being a part of social groups functioning around you. You get to know more people, and it provides an opportunity to work with those with whom you live.

The point of building social skills is not always about the big promotion at the office. You'll also learn to tackle clients no matter which field of work you are in. Working with people enables you to learn their characteristics and traits. Hence, you may take time to manage your clients, but you will learn something new with each experience.

Personality tests, job interviews, and public speaking will not be as tough as they seemed earlier. Your friendly personality, body language, eye contact, confidence, social skills, and easy expressions can prove that you are not under pressure in social settings. This is a big thumbs up because people like working with those who are approachable and have a good attitude.

When you are part of the social system and step forward to help others, others are bound to help you as well. What goes around comes around, so your kindness may return in other forms.

From the Author's Life

Virtual friendships can either be very special or lead you to a pool of problems. When they fall somewhere between these two extremes, it is safe and not quite bothersome. I remember the time when I was young and had an online friend. Back then, it used to be the highlight of my day. I remember the excitement I'd feel from seeing her email notification and the anticipation of her letter response to my previous letter. The scenario where you are exported to another world through a string of words is indeed possible, and the internet does make it feasible and popular today. There are so many of us who would hesitate to come across and say "hello," but, today, the internet can help us shed this shyness, so much so that we must muster enough courage to post a happy picture or a selfie. While it can be very normal for most people, posting a photo online can still be anxiety-inducing for those like us. This is also often seen as a new stressor, because while many get hundreds of likes on their photos, some of us wonder if we will ever reach a fraction of that amount. In terms of friendships, I speak of likes and comments because we miss out on any genuine care and excitement in online conversations today. Rather, we aim to impress people to befriend them.

Most young teenagers today have a social media account. Having an active, attractive, and updated social media profile is central to gaining more friends. This is true for young adults as well. Posting pictures that show how socially active you are is one way to tell the world that you have a happy and fulfilled life. And not just that—the social media aspect also shows a person's interests, hobbies, and talents. For any generation who cannot relate, what getting a new haircut or buying a new dress was for you back in your day is the same as posting a new picture and liked on a social media account. How many likes and comments one receives is akin to how socially approved, accepted, and appreciated an individual is.

But there is another significant angle to social media and an important one. The Internet gives us an easy way to come together for a valuable or noble cause. It can move communities, wake people up, bring protestors together, and help us ask all the right questions. It is possible for people to meet on such platforms and build strong camaraderie. But it isn't just about these strong serious social causes. If we look at the gaming community, as an example, many members are acquainted with each other even if they have not met each other in person. Then, there is another beautiful aspect to social media: social interactions through motivating each other and inspiring each other. There are many groups advocating mental health issues that bring people together, both virtually and in person. We must also take into account the fact that not all follows and likes on social media are superficial. There are people who genuinely care and make efforts to stay connected. There are people who inspire each other through friendships that start out as long distance eventually turn into beautiful, long-term bonds. This does not mean everyone who sends you a "hello" in an online messaging platform can be trusted. It is just that some people may be more comfortable beginning a friendship online because the first step makes reaching out easier than walking up to a person and starting a conversation. The fear of rejection or being made fun of is a real fear, and the virtual world offers a way to be connected to people with common interests, hobbies, and causes without the repercussions.

However, some of the downside one may face online includes grooming, catfishing, identity theft, bullying, online harassment, isolation, betrayal of trust, and emotional abuse. Not all virtual connections lead to genuine emotional bonds. It's not impossible, but while reluctance in real life is an understood cause of emotional discontinuity when forming new friendships, some regulation and caution must be an accepted norm and should be practiced when forming new friendships online. Because hiding behind a social media profile and acting on a whim is easier, but so is hiding in anonymity and winning a naive person's trust. It is easier to choose and drop friends online just as it is being a closed-off person in real life. In a nutshell, I think there is definitely a place for virtual friendships, but it comes with a bigger element of risk. So, for a healthy social life, this medium should be in addition to, rather than a replacement for, the real world.

Food for Thought

If you do initiate contact, how do you choose to do it and why? By calling, dropping by, or texting them?

An option to consider:

This should really depend on what the dynamics with your friend are like. Not everyone is okay with talking via text message; some need you to pick up the phone and call them because they consider it a more dignified way to interact. But there are also people who hate to talk on the phone or meet in person not because they are not interested in talking to you but because they genuinely do not have time to sit and talk. For the latter, every minute of their lives is precious. In any case, interacting should come naturally to you and your friend. There have to be no forced engagements. You would know this when you decide to talk to them. However, interactions can be initiated from one side but have to always be maintained from both sides. If you feel that your effort is being wasted and you are continuously ignored, you should stop and let your friend initiate the interaction. Some friendships die for no reason, but there are many more people around, and just one conversation can change the course of your friendship—for the better, of course—with them.

Chapter 3:
Introverts, Extroverts, Ambiverts, and Omniverts

True happiness does not lie in making many friends. True happiness comes with being happy with self. Inculcating self-care and healthy habits can save us on days when we have to be dependent on ourselves. These can help you on days when you are looking for a creative outlet to release pent-up emotions or when you have no one around. It's days like these that test our patience and resolve. Our agenda to make friends should not be to be happy; instead, it's to have a group of people, albeit small, who are reliable, honest, caring, and fun to be with. When choosing friends, it is we who should define and declare these parameters. Your criteria for fun can be very different from mine. If you are into books, chances are that you can meet new people at the local library or at a book club. If you are into a certain genre of music, you can make friends at a studio or at a concert. If you are into fitness, you can forge new friendships at a gym or even on an online fitness-conscious group.

Some friendships fail because people expect more than these relationships can provide. Expecting happiness from a relationship places too much pressure on the other person. A person who knows their boundaries and what makes them content is more balanced and their expectations are more realistic. Their relationships are more stable because they focus on the needs of both sides. If you are happy with your life, you will not look for excuses to blame someone else if unhappiness surfaces. An ungrateful person will look for reasons to play the blame game. They are never happy in their relationships because they are never happy with themselves. This does not mean we are wrong to expect what is fair. Fair treatment is a basic right in all friendships. One can never truly connect with someone if there is no trust, dignity, or understanding between two people. Some of us pull down walls that guard us to become more vulnerable. Some basic expectations are always just. This is why the first things we need to ask when we look at ourselves in the mirror every morning are

- How happy are we really?
- How well do we treat ourselves?
- What purpose do our new friends serve in our life?

Why Do Some People Struggle to Make Friends?

There are many people who would like to be more connected to others but struggle to do so. They are empathetic and understand other people's experiences well. Yet, when it comes to expressing their own thoughts and feelings in front of others, even the people they know well, they seem to face a problem. Such shy people may often be introverted. It is a result of their developing years and is now a part of who they are. Their interactions with their parents may be limited, which may have led to limited interactions with others as well. What these people have learned from their environment and how they reacted to it also play a role in modeling their behavior. Some people have a natural tendency to be shy, others have learned to be shy with experience, and some are also shy because they do not like surprises. Thus, they tread a cautious path, carefully gaining comfort and confidence with each step they take, because being coerced into doing something is not their style. Some unfortunate experiences like bullying or teasing also make people confide in no one.

Is Your Shyness Your Weakness?

Some introverts would like to believe that being shy is a disadvantage. However, there is something about the quiet strength that is innate to shy people that may be lacking in others. Not being too outspoken isn't always bad. It's also a myth that introverts cannot have many friends. On the contrary, people who stay quiet are better listeners. They are sensitive, caring, and protective. Introverts may have few friends, but they have few *good* friends. It is their ability to relate to other people's feelings that make them some of the most reliable people. Hence, even with limited social skills and a tendency to open up slowly, some people can succeed in making friends.

Shyness can be due to various reasons that don't always revolve around discomfort, nervousness, fear, insecurity, and self-consciousness. Not all shy people blush or feel shaky when talking to others. Some people prefer being shy. They are comfortable not uttering a word in front of others but are capable of expressing themselves through outlets like poetry or stage performance. This stands true even for celebrities, who could be very popular yet still be shy. The deal is to not let your introversion become your disability. There is nothing wrong with you being an introvert.

Understanding the Four Personality Types

Investing our time in understanding other people's personalities helps us not only to know them better but also to delve deeper into our own personality type. In fact, learning everything about ourselves, from eccentricities to self-reliance, helps us to live a more authentic life. This becomes important when we want to genuinely connect with others because we cannot fake connections; our bonds are not made with shallowness in our hearts. No matter what is one's personality type, authenticity is a quality that is always sought after, be it in friendships or leadership. Authentic people are the ones who have the quality to be true and the courage to be real. They do not copy others, and neither do they hide personality traits to look different from who they truly are. Embracing who we are is the first step to acceptance of the self and gaining confidence.

Instead of nitpicking details about ourselves, we can attempt to understand what shapes us. In this chapter, we aim to discuss the four personality types. No person ever is painted in one color. We are all various shades of all these four personalities.

Introverts

The literal meaning of "intro-" (inward) "-vert" (turn) means to turn inwards. The act of introverting means turning inwards. Introverts are usually turned upon themselves, which means that their personality is focused more on their own inner world than the outer world. These people may be shy, reserved, quiet, and private.

Making Friends as an Introvert

As an introvert, you need to accept that talking to others and opening up does not come naturally to you and may be a massive disadvantage when making friends. But there is a massive advantage, too. Because you are slow and cautious, you choose your friends wisely and freely. You are under no pressure to be part of a social group just because they look happy and you are desperate to gain friends. This saves you because the friends you make can be your long-term pals. These are the people you choose after you place trust in them. Another massive positive to your personality is that you see things that others do not. This means you observe minute details that others may overlook. This gives you the added benefit of noticing the details. You can address them, and you can also use them when trying to build a potential friendship.

You can begin with learning to accept that your hobbies and interests may be the same others have, but the way you nurture them could be a little different. However, this creates a great opportunity to meet new people. Hobbies allow us to make new friends because we tend to be inclined toward people with similar interests. It is a lot easier to initiate a conversation about something that you know or want to learn about. Creative people can involve other people through art, sportspeople through fitness and discipline, booklovers through book clubs, and so on. Communities never fail you, and while trusting one person can take time, making a couple of friends somewhere you all can meet is a win-win for everyone.

Another thing you can do as an introvert is to develop new interests. Trying a new hobby, like attending a cooking or baking class, can place you in a more social, friendlier, and comfortable atmosphere. You remain in your comfort zone while stepping out of it. This is also a great way to find new opportunities and let life happen to you. Where there are people, making at least one friend shouldn't be very hard.

However, being around more people can overwhelm some introverts, too. Suddenly foraging into the crowd can make us feel lost and anxious. Just because everyone from your new zumba class has decided to go and watch a film after class doesn't mean you do have to tag along—at least, not yet. Take your time. There's no need to close your eyes and take a deep plunge. You can sit at home in your pajamas and watch a show or just chat with someone online. Online groups help people connect from their isolated hubs.

You can also reconnect with old friends who you feel understood you better than others. You may have lost touch with them for some reason or another, but do not hesitate to reach out. For some introverts, talking to someone they're familiar with is easier than talking to a complete stranger. First moves can make us nervous, but there are more chances to succeed in such a case than when approaching someone you barely know.

Even when you want to reach out to people you may know, blindly trusting them is a task close to impossible. Even so, it's better to look around yourself and see if there's anyone you would like to get to know better. Chances are that you will find such people. It is the same drill: Do not be afraid to reach out, and even before that, you might want to know them better from a distance. For example, who are the people they hang out with? What are their interests? Do you have any mutual friends? This can give you a better idea about who they are and if they would want to be your friends as well, as friendships are not one-sided. People look for solid reasons to make new friends, and if you have none, why would they want to get to know you? On the contrary, your friends can introduce you to their friends. This is the easiest and safest way to connect with more people, and that too at the pace you like.

It takes time to make new friends, so don't ask for anyone's number or address out of the blue. If you rush it, you can ruin it. Let others know you better and invite you more. Everything gets better with time. But, above all, do not lose your identity. Your uniqueness must be preserved at all costs. Do not think about changing yourself, your ideas, interests, thoughts, and behavior for others, and you shouldn't feel bad if others didn't invite you just because you declined an event invite earlier. You should not apologize for being yourself. People who appreciate you will also respect your choices and decisions.

Extroverts

These people are often described as the life of a party. They come early with a bunch of friends and leave late with a bigger group of friends. No matter which event they attend, there are always people who know them already. They have an outgoing, relaxed, vibrant, and confident persona that attracts people to them, but extroverts are not always attracted toward other extroverts. It is a myth that extroverts and introverts cannot be friends. While extroverts love interactions, they also need to retreat into their shell when it's time to recharge their battery. There are many extroverts who like to go on solo adventure trips or to a theater to watch a film alone. This is because as much as they like social interaction, their inner selves also demand peace and tranquility, and they get this by spending some time alone. This is their way of turning their attention onto themselves, their needs, and clearing out their space. These people also enjoy interacting with strangers. So while they are away from their usual group of friends, one never knows they might be bonding and making new friends to whichever destination they have traveled to.

Extroverts can also be unpredictable. Today, they might be working at a great place and living their best life, and tomorrow, they may suddenly quit everything to live a secluded life in the mountains or somewhere surrounded by nature. Their engagement in various social activities keeps them fulfilled and rejuvenated. According to Carl Jung, the famous psychologist, extroverts derived their energy from crowds and the world around them; on the other hand, introverts were the total opposite (Roy, n.d.). Being an extrovert doesn't mean that a person cannot live a quiet life. While introverts cannot be extroverts, some extroverts are introverted during certain times or when needs arise. Extroversion is an entire spectrum, introversion is at one polar end of it. There are many reasons why people may feel more extroverted than others, and these may include their upbringing, hormones, and even genetic makeup.

Extroverts can be people who enjoy social gatherings. These are people who like to be the center of attention at parties. Social stimulation is necessary for them in the absence of which they may feel isolated, dejected, afraid, and anxious. They are unafraid of new and unfamiliar social situations and avail the opportunities to introduce themselves and make social connections. They may have some alone time, but they'll gradually come out of their shell to return into society and mingle with friends and colleagues. These are the people who can even stay back after an intense meeting and plan an after-work party. Not only do they thrive in such social settings, but they also lead the group and plan all the group activities. It is them who decides where to go, where to eat, and where to party. They love invitations and hardly turn them down. If you are an introvert, having an extrovert friend can be of great help. They know a lot of people, and finding friends through them may be easier.

Because extroverts make friends easily, they initiate conversations easily, too. They enjoy the energy they feel at social gatherings and engaging with new people. The sole purpose behind this interaction is expanding their social circle. They believe in discussing any problems rather than hiding them or brushing them under the carpet. This upfront behavior earns them many fans, too. They do not internalize any issue; they discuss it and seek solutions. They do not mind asking for help readily when in trouble because they do not fear being judged. Because they are so willing to cooperate with others, they are clear about what they want and why. They know why they are socializing with a certain person, and this gives them a fresh perspective on things and also helps them to make better choices in life.

Their optimism, positivity, cheerfulness, and adaptable behavior helps them to view the good side of things and not dwell on negativity. They also believe in taking risks to expand both business and benefits. Not all risks are successful, but when they are, they can excite the mind and make it more confident and elated. This further pushes the risk-taking tendency of a person. These rewards are stimulating for the brain as well.

Ambiverts vs. Omniverts

Ambiverts are the people who have reached a balance between their introverted and extroverted tendencies. These people are spontaneous, but they are also cautious. They are organized and disciplined while also able to enjoy thrill and adventure. Omniverts, on the other hand, do not show any tendency. They are neither mood nor personality dependent, but they are situation dependent. These two personalities do not feel the pressure to fit into the mold. They work what is in their best interest.

A person who can balance their introversion and extroversion to make enough friends while also enjoying considerable alone time is called an *ambivert*. They have friends and are outgoing. They prefer social isolation in some instances without being antisocial people. Ambiverts have more chances of success and leadership than extroverts because their lack of social interactions do not eat them up. A lack of friends is not their immediate social crisis, and moving to a new city or joining a new office is not that big a problem for them. They are not scared of social rejection. They are comfortable in their skin and thrive by separating themselves from the "introvert" and "extrovert" tags.

Omniverts break the introversion and extroversion ceiling and are courageous enough to try what works best for them. How we deal with these pressures, in turn, determines how we interact with others around us. Ambiverts learn to balance this pressure. This can make things steady and consistent for them. On the other hand, omniverts learn to adjust themselves to this pressure. Even in the face of extreme introversion and extroversion, one can switch their personality to suit the situation. Although, unlike ambiverts, omniverts do not balance their shyness and friendliness too well. This dual personality trait, which is not balanced, can lead to extreme highs and lows in their mood (Miller, 2023). For example, one minute they could be a public figure, facing the media and maintaining their calm, and another minute, they can be at a private dinner sharing their childhood memories with guests.

From the Author's Life

I agree when people say we should not label anyone. Labels can be deceptive. When you first get to know me on the surface, you would think I am extroverted. That is because I can talk to people, I like talking to people, and I am comfortable talking to people. It's only when people get closer to me do they realize that I am equally introverted. Just because I do not act as an introvert, it does not mean that I am not shy. I have always been shy. I like being by myself, and there are very few people whose company I enjoy. I am good with people because I don't mind company. But am I comfortable with a large group of people on a daily basis? No, especially not when I have to prepare a project with them, or when I'm presenting a paper or giving a presentation. I am also not very fond of big social gatherings. I would rather prefer a small, closely knit group of friends. I am most comfortable being alone, and I attend events, functions, and gatherings when I am ready.

The trick is to prepare oneself mentally, and I'm fortunate that I can do that easily. Not everyone can do that, and I understand the inability and distress that comes with it because introverted people need company, too. We are also so blown away by the idea that we all need friends—which is true, by the way—that we think we need to depend on someone. To some extent, yes, we all need to depend on someone, but circumstances do not always let us do that. In a world that is overpopulated, it is quite ironic that so many of us lack what we call "true friendships." Socializing, hence, is a required skill to survive. I remember I knew someone who would visit a coffee shop every evening only to talk to the owner. For the time that I stayed in this new city, I used to visit this place for my coffee on most evenings. Each day that I visited this place, I would find this old man sitting at the counter, chatting away with the owner. His dog would sit quietly beside his feet. Their ritual was to watch the news together, talk about—I suppose, because I did not understand the language, barring a few words—politics, weather, their neighborhood, gossip, and then they'd stand at the stairs and smoke for a while. Imagine that being the highlight of your evening—seeing your friend daily and living an easy and peaceful life, just watching time pass by. And, if that wasn't enough, the view was beautiful. The place smelled of fresh buns and cakes, cocoa, and coffee. Although I have visited many places for work and pleasure, this small peaceful town, which was away from city noise, filled my heart to the brim with fuzzy feelings. I often think about those two men; I think about them, their lives, and if they still meet. I really hope so, because in that small coffee shop, I saw what friendship meant. No matter how big an introvert you might be, such small innocent instances make you crave human connection. We do not need many people or a lot of money to be happy. We just want one person who waits for us every evening, and just one person who arrives every evening that we wait for them. That is all that there is to friendship.

Food for Thought

One of your closest friends has her birthday party. She has a large social circle and invites you and your best friend as well. Your best friend, who has just moved to the city, is very shy and quiet. She adores your friend but is not motivated enough to attend the party with you. While your best friend is not antisocial, she is not fond of parties. You do not want to leave her but you also do not want to miss the party. What would you do?

An option to consider:

Attending the party is your friend's call. It is true that a place crowded with people, where everyone knows everyone else, can be intimidating for those who prefer smaller gatherings. At the most, you can make sure that your friend feels included in your presence. Since she decided to attend the party, you can introduce her to like-minded people and give her company. This doesn't necessarily mean that you have to exclude yourself from all the fun, but you would have to be kind to her needs and sensitive to her approach. It takes time even for the most social people to make friends in a new setting. You play the balancing act here because not attending your friend's party would be rude, and not taking your friend along with you would be rude as well. See yourself as half the host who is not just bringing a friend to a party but bringing her best friend to meet her closest friend and her other friends. They're not all bound to like each other, though this can be a great opportunity for all of you to have some fun and get to know each other better.

Chapter 4:
Understanding Who You Are as a Person

Soul-stirring conversations do not happen out of the blue. They are initiated as normal conversations, and they take turns, visit "creases," and make you think hard. They can be so mentally captivating that you love it and want the conversation going forever. It is not a one-way delivery. You are not listening to one person speak in a conversation. There is always a more than one-person narrative. This possibility and the existence of multiple dialogues and multiple narratives means respect and tolerance for each other's opinions. Friendship is only possible when this bonhomie is not fake. It does not matter if you are up all night talking about films; neither does it matter when you all sit up to talk about wars. What matters is how comfortable you all are in each other's company.

Friendships occur between two or among multiple people. Sometimes you need to take the lead. Other times, you need to sit back and allow your friend to just be.

No matter how experienced one is, it is natural to feel panic when expected to network or meet new clients. One can practice as much as they want, but every situation is new, and there are numerous new ways to begin a conversation. Then, there are those kids who sit in the back of the class, reticent, reclusive, with too many thoughts in their heads, and too many dreams seem impossible. These kids are those who aren't ignored in class; to ignore someone, you have to see someone first. These are kids who go unseen. No one likes them, no one talks to them, and no one invites them to join in on activities. What should be their career choice? What should they do to have a different life? Is the onus solely on them to make perfect choices that end their agony? The weariness that comes with self-consciousness, awkwardness, and nervousness never allows us to be optimal when it comes to learning social skills. Then, there are people who were once very social, but something kept them aloof for certain periods of their life. It could be marriage, a child, a peculiar job, health issues, or other personal causes. Coming back to socializing agony may be difficult even for those who had no problem talking to people before.

The Power That Comes With Knowing Yourself

Understanding who you are as a person has everything to do with being self-aware. But making friends is not always about what the other person feels or does. It has a lot to do with the ways you positively change their lives. This is where self-awareness helps. It is wrong to feel dejected and unappreciated just because we feel ignored. Reality does not always transpire and reach us correctly.

When we are not approached by anyone, we feel miserable. We feel we are the odd ones left out because maybe we come across as annoying, of the way we look, or we are destined to be alone forever. Everyone else seems to be having friends and enjoying life. Making the first move is almost humiliating, because initiating a connection is also about prestige for most people: *Why should I make the first move? I should be good enough to attract people. Why should I go to someone's table and introduce myself? What if I am rejected? What if I am made fun of?* It is very normal to have fears like these. However, once you know how to approach someone and you've managed to approach them, you'd know it was never about them. Sure, they had your attention, and maybe they had other people's attention, too, but they never made a move themselves because they were probably more shy than you were. Once you meet them, you would know how delighted they are to meet you and how glad and grateful they are to know you.

We dwell too much on details that do not matter. It can be at extremes for some people. Some may not want to go out and meet anyone at all. On the other hand, some people want to go out of their way to prove their love and loyalty to people who matter to them. Both these extremes come with their harms. There is never a need to prove to anyone how much they matter to us; it is evident in how we treat them every day. There is also no need to do something grand to make up for the days we ignored them, as it should never come to the point that someone feels ignored. These are little things we need to know about our personalities when trying to socialize with others. We cannot be more wrong about our personality and behavior at any point in life. This is where we need to turn our thinking around. We need to move from finding flaws within ourselves where it does not matter to finding areas where we can make positive changes.

Have you ever noticed why so many talented, wonderful, intelligent, and educated people are incredibly shy? Do you ever think, *Thank god I approached this person or this wonderful human may not have entered*? Trust me, there'll be times when you'll be bursting with happiness that you made the first move, and this is why, while we need to polish certain parts of our personality to attract others, we need to also remember that attracting someone is just one aspect of our personality. Knowing someone better to be friends with them—if there is a connection at all—is work at a much deeper level. That is, it involves your psyche and values as well.

But it is this first step that's a major hurdle for most of us. Beyond this, we as people are craving deeper connections and meaningful friendships. Why does small talk seem like too small a task to even consider? What is its use? And why should one learn it?

The Art and Skill of Small Talk

Now, before I begin this, I need to explain why I was talking about personality and the energy one brings with their persona. When we say "small talk," we generally think of statements like

- "Hi!"
- "Hello!"
- "How are you?"
- "What do you do?"
- "Where are you from?"
- "Where do you work?"

These are generic statements, and they are good when initially getting to know someone. What about after this? This is not the greatest beginning to any conversation, but this is how we learned to talk the old-school way. It is not just an art but also a fascinating skill, yet we need to understand in what ways our personality matches someone else's personality so that it can lead to a memorable conversation and cherished bond. First of all, casual conversations that happen all throughout the day are no different than the small talk you have with a stranger. It is our overthinking that has separated and categorized the sentences we exchange. To some people, these conversations happen almost naturally. They speak as if they have done this a zillion times before, but you feel your conversations evaporate as soon as they've begun. To correct this, you don't have to find flaws in yourself; rather, change your perspective. A meaningful dialogue continues because both parties are interested and want to remain engaged. Secondly, a dying conversation can always be resuscitated. Do not start dreading already just because the other person seems disinterested. Maybe they don't know what to say, they don't know enough about the topic to respond, they want to talk about something else, or they are just shy. Thirdly, it's easy to transition from one topic to another, but it generally depends on the mood, the location, the circumstances in which you two have met, and your goal behind this connection. Fourthly, if it's an informal event or a party, you should be more relaxed. Fifthly, always end the conversation with grace even if you do not intend to stay friends with this person. This is because you never know when you might bump into them again. You also do not know if you can get to know more interesting people through this one contact. And, finally, you should not end things based on your opinions formed in just one meeting.

How you treat others can make a person feel valued and included. This is something they would remember for a very long time, and if they see you again, chances are they would come to talk to you. All the people who you see smiling and conversing comfortably also began their journey this way. They don't know everyone, nor were they always this popular. Gaining friends takes a long time. Even for natural-born talkers, it is not easy to earn friends. It takes practice, attention, patience, and learning.

There are no rules, but imagine a scenario where you know two shopkeepers. There is one who is an acquaintance. There is another who you do not know. They both sell their garments at the same price offering you the same discount rate. Now, chances are that most of you will go to the person you know better than the person you don't know at all. This is because you mark your presence where you feel friendly and welcomed. It is not purely business tactics that always win. There are also chances that the person you know may give you additional discounts on the promise that you will bring your friends to their shop or that you'll come back soon to buy more things. This is also a great deal because it is possible to run into them again and converse. Leaving it on a bitter note by buying something from their competitor does not earn you a new friend, but it makes you lose a potential friend. This is why small talk is necessary. When you talk about where you live, what you do, and why you two should be connected, it's easy to only think of the ways you two can benefit each other.

If I were a wholesale dealer of paint, I would like to know shopkeepers who sell paint and related products. If I'm a freelancer, I would like to personally know all my clients so that they return to me when they need the type of service I provide. If I were a school teacher, getting to know the parents can help both parties to understand how we can add positive values to the life and career of a student and bring out the best in them. This is also great for the reviews and future opportunities in my career that I'd receive. In today's world of high technology and high tension, all we crave are high connections. High connections add more to our life. They do not eat away our valuable time or place us in miserable positions. These are the people we go out of our comfort zone to meet. Sheryl, who shifted to a new neighborhood, still drives to her old one to get all the groceries. Why? Because that is where she brought groceries from for the last ten years and she likes the people there. Penelope's mother drives an hour to see her dentist because he is the one she trusts even though there are two A-list dentists on the same route. People talk, meet, and relate to humanize their existence. Sam likes to call the same man to mow his lawn because they chat while he does his work. He always liked him. He felt he was honest, dignified, and sensible. This is something Sam can do on his own, but he had called this man, Chris, the first time when Sam had broken his leg. Chris was not just friendly; after mowing the lawn, he made some tea and the two men sat and talked about everything under the sun. That was five years ago around when Sam had lost his wife to an accident—the same that had broken his leg. While people came and grieved, all of them went away. They all said they were sorry for Sam's loss, although it was not just any loss. Sam felt he had lost his reason to live, but he had another reason: his daughter, Donna. Interestingly, Chris had a girl, Jessica, who was the same age. Donna and Jessica bonded just as their fathers did. Through a job, a few conversations, and some evenings, Sam and Donna found a family in their new friends.

Words do not just fill a void that hangs in the air. They do not just fill the silence. Meaningful words from people who you share meaningful friendships with can solve problems and fulfill needs. It always feels positive to gain good friends and small talk is usually the beginning of it. With the right words, we can approach people easily and leave a positive impression, too. Convincing someone can also begin with just small talk. You visit a store to buy a washing machine. You see various models and choose the one that best fits your needs, but who convinces you to buy it? The one whose words evoke a positive reaction from you, someone who is a great conversationalist—the right salesman. It is ultimately your choice where to spend the money, but talking is a major deal because it influences your choices.

In a world that can be fast, brutally unkind, and unforgiving, repeating the same sentences will not interest someone who feels they have battled with the world. If a child, who probably faces exclusion at school or is finding their studies difficult, returns home to answer "how was your day" on an everyday basis, they will either break down someday or learn to lie to avoid hurting their parents' feelings. They may try not to break down so as to not feel humiliated, and they would neither be able to lie for too long, so the best they can manage is to generally avoid their parents' conversations. And this is something that adults do, too. I do not want to talk about my interests when all I can think of is leaving the party immediately to be back home by 11. I wouldn't stop to get to know someone better unless they're interesting enough to have all my attention.

The bridge that is built between two people has a lot to do with both the tone and language that's used. Words can fill the void, but what if they never reach the other person? That bridge is bound to go down.

Small Talk to Make the Other Person Feel Great

To know someone else, you need to know yourself better. What are the questions you would like to answer at a party? Where do you work? No, not really—at least, not always, unless it's a business party, and you're looking for potential clients. Personally, I think that if I attend a housewarming party after a long day, I wouldn't want to talk about how terrible my day was and how mean my boss usually is.

There are many ways to initiate or join a conversation. If you feel someone is making a valid point, you can always gently interrupt to support them. This is not an interruption they would mind:

- "I agree with you on this."
- "I think you are right."
- "That's a valid point."
- "True!"

This encourages the other person to smile and pause for you to say more. If you suddenly feel the limelight is on you, you can go on and say, "I just felt you were right, and I didn't mean to interrupt you. Please go on." This is one way to mark your presence at a gathering.

If you don't know how to initiate a conversation, you can always join in on it. Small talk can help us to be a part of an ongoing conversation:

- "I've lived briefly in Denver. I loved my time there."
- "Oh, you paint?! That's wonderful! I would love to see your work someday."
- "The weather is good today. I feel like going on a long drive."

Find a way to connect people and their names with an ongoing conversation. *Never* call a person by the wrong name. If you are not sure, do not be shy to ask a person's name twice. They would never mind it as much as they would mind you calling them by a wrong name:

- "I'm sorry, I've forgotten your name."
- "Can you tell me your name again, please?"
- "Excuse me, I think I got your name wrong. What's your name again?"

Never fail to smile or greet the other, even if you have missed their name. You can always say, "I know we've met somewhere, but I don't remember where." Another thing you can do is to take the initiative to introduce two people. For example, if you are at a table at a social gathering where you have just met a person, and another stranger walks up to you two to feel welcomed and included, be the one in charge: "Hello, my name is Linda. This is Amber. What's your name?"

When trying to genuinely compliment someone, do not use a tag. "Debbie, you are awesome" is always better than "Debra, you are funny." Part of trying to make new friends also includes reconnecting with them while allowing them to feel relevant:

- "Susan, what was the name of the band you told me about last week?"
- "Hello, Katherine. I heard your sister was in an accident. How is she now?"
- "Hey, Adam. It's been so long. Want to catch up soon?"
- "Wow, Patrick! How do you know so much about astrology?"

From the Author's Life

I should talk about an incident that includes my mother's very good friend, and a pediatrician, Victoria. I remember going to Vicky's clinic once because I needed to deliver a package, and I was running late for my music class. Instead of going to her home, I decided to see her directly at her office. Vicky's assistant was getting a shot ready for a little four-year-old who was there with her parents. When I got there, Vicky was talking to the child and explaining everything in detail to her. I was horrified to see a three-year-old being told why she was being given the medicine as an injection. I distinctly remember the child asking, "Will it hurt?"

Vicky replied, "Well, if you listen to me properly and follow my instructions, then it won't."

"But will it hurt?" she asked again.

Vicky's reply was, "It may if you do not listen to me."

I was, of course, running late, so I left with the child's image of clutching her soft toy tightly.

A few days later, I met Vicky over family lunch and asked her everything about that appointment. "Oh, yes, I intend to be very honest with little kids because sometimes they have to see me again, and I don't think lying is the best first impression when I am trying to be their friend." I laughed out a little too loud because I didn't think anything near to friendship even stood a chance between Vicky and a child, but then my mom reminded me of how I always felt comfortable going to Vicky as a kid.

"But that was because I knew her," I retorted back.

"No, that was because you trusted her and saw a friend in her."

Maybe she was right. Vicky's clinic was very child friendly. "So do you still sing to your little patients?" I winked at Auntie Vicky.

She replied, "My singing's so bad that it hurts, so yes, comparatively, the injection does hurt less. Hey, I intend to keep my promise to my new friends."

Whoever says singing is not a part of small talk did not know the rules, and rule number one—the only rule to making small talk—is that there are no rules. You have to just be yourself.

Food for Thought

Your friend is always supportive, but they tend to become a bit overcritical at some points. While they always push you to be your best self and achieve success, they undermine your qualities of empathy, kindness, understanding, and truthfulness. They crossed a line today, and that really hurt you. While they were trying to be honest with you, you felt you needed a break. How do you confront this situation?

An option to consider:

Honesty is appreciated in friendships. Do not be afraid of being labeled "sensitive" when being honest. When you're with a friend you trust, you should be allowed to be your authentic self. If being overcritical is how they are, you have the right to be who you are; a true friendship would never be affected by that. No two people need to censor themselves, and you should not try to change them nor allow them to change you. If your soft side bothers them and they still want to be your friend, they will learn to live with it. If their overcritical side bothers you, but your friend is dear to you, you will learn to live with this tiny little flaw. I have seen people grow with each other to the extent that major flaws become minor personality issues. We learn to live with our friends and who they are as a whole. But if you feel that you are not respected or valued or feel ridiculed or attacked to a painful extent, even after you chose to be vulnerable, the onus of maintaining the friendship does not lie on you. Yes, your friend may have supported you innumerable times, but constantly telling you that you are flawed is continually pulling you down, and you should choose peace and not pain in such situations.

Chapter 5:
Navigating Social Situations and Overcoming Social Anxiety

Earlier, kids used to befriend other kids at school or on the playground. As time passed, these friendships faded. Today, there are so many places where kids meet and make friends. There are ways to stay in touch even when the possibility of physically meeting disappears. But our kids are more isolated than we were in our childhood. The world of kids is no different from the world of adults when it comes to making social connections. They emulate us. But every time we make a friend, we take a chance. We do not have to be excessively outgoing to make friends. Consistent attempts at trying to reach out to people may seem tiring and unproductive, but it is not something you do for others; it is something you do for yourself.

Adults have a greater sense of self-awareness than kids, which is both a good and bad thing. With more awareness, some of us are also more self-conscious. Kids do not judge. They just take the plunge. They would go and shake hands with the one they like. They will say "hello" with a smile. We grow older to wrap ourselves in a false image. This image is laden with insecurities. What if the other person does not smile back? Let's be honest, it is not a big deal if the other person does not smile back. If someone does not respond to your hello, that is okay, too. The sky would not fall. Just as kids move on and continue playing, we need to move on, too. Yet, our brain gets too stuck on one incident where our "hello" was not returned.

The first step to regaining confidence in self and social connections around us is by letting go of the fears that crowd our minds. For those people whose lives are on the verge of collapsing, what is stopping you from interacting with others? Yes, there could be many who would not return you a smile but there would be some who would. Mastering social skills is not just about smiling with a "hello." It is all about conducting social experiments and finding out which one works the best for you.

Understanding the Reverse Psychology of Friendship

Ethics has a special place in relationships. Friendship is one stream of relationships that can be so strong, it may pull strangers to become a family. We do not just call anyone our friend. Friendships are personal and important. For some people, these can be life-changing. As they're mostly based on the concerns you have for the other person due to the intimate bond you share with them, there are no trade-ups in friendships. What matters more are the values two people share and how they decide to stick to these values. There is mutual care and some shared activity that is fun to be delved into. This distinction is reason enough to call two people friends. Imagine sharing with someone the thoughts that are in your mind. You do this because you know you have a confidant, but this would make sense only when the affection is reciprocated. Unrequited friendships are more conceptual and less practical than unrequited love. Friendships are never one sided. This is a basic principle of all friendships. We make friends for

- camaraderie
- values
- support

You may want to be friends with someone for how they attract and interest you. You may be impressed by them and the idea of being their friend excites you. They fit in your idea of fun. They may also look like an escape route from your difficult and tedious life. Then, come those friends who share your virtues. These are the people who inspire you through their character. Their values make them extraordinary, and you feel any healthy association with them can help you bring some light to your life. You know that this friendship would be appreciated by your friends, family, and colleagues as it can elevate you in society. It could be for a cause or for status. However, there is one kind of friendship, the third kind, that is supposed to last the longest. When you are friends with someone for support, you tend to be committed forever. This is true for strong friendships that are equal and reciprocal from both sides. It is not a give-and-take situation where you both help each other because you owe it. There is a mature understanding that you both are in this together and ought to help each other out whenever needed. The simple reason being, you both matter to each other. No other friendship, be it for fun or virtues, can be functional for too long without support. Friendships that are supportive exhibit a broader construct for dialogue. There is

- mutual respect
- mutual care
- intimacy
- trust
- shared interests, morals, and ideals

What Do You Bring to the Table?

When we are talking about attracting friends, we need to introspect what we have to offer to new friends. Is our character strong enough to inspire others? Do our actions align with the values we talk about? How do we plan to charm others? Are we helpful enough? Are we reluctant in new friendships? Do we have trust issues? How do we approach a new friend? Do we have all the qualities that we look for in our friends?

When introverts want to be friends with a new person, most of them are scared to approach this new situation out of fear of rejection. Extroverts, on the other hand, move ahead with optimism for fear of losing out on an opportunity. In both cases, our focus is on the other person and what they have to contribute to our lives. We try to give our best impression, whether we approach them or not. The story does not end at this first impression. Being authentic has less to do with what our personality is like and more with how we see a friendship. This is another reason why an introvert can very easily be friends with an extrovert. If these two have found the support they had been looking for and lacking all the while, they can connect instantly. Friendships are not limited to shared interests and hobbies; they are also bound with shared safe spaces and shared silences. When two people trust each other's presence, they are unafraid to be vulnerable.

Finding the Right Tribe

Shyness, social anxieties, and insecurities can discourage us from opening up to others. These conditions come with various nuances and their effects are different on different people, but, overall, they cause social awkwardness and discomfort in people. From being severely withdrawn to being mildly shy, there is an entire range with regard to how we act and react when shy.

Countering the Mental Barriers

The biggest side effect of shyness is how it alters our thinking patterns. The hesitant, untalkative, meek behavior gives off unfriendly vibes. But, more than that, shy people begin to believe that talking to others is a huge risk, so much so that they don't believe any compliments that come their way and any joy in socializing has lost its appeal. Self-doubt and inhibitions cloud their minds, creating weak first impressions on others. It can wreck a person's confidence and even make them less ambitious. Making friends may take longer because there is a sense of loss of control. Trusting others takes longer, too.

Add social anxiety to this mess. There is always a disbalance in cognitive reasoning when one is anxious; there is no logical or objective reasoning. It fuels our insecurities and self-doubts and discourages us from doing better. The willingness to be our best selves is constantly hindered by unpleasant and nervous disputative and disruptive thoughts. When in social situations, we pose the other person as a threat. Our emotions may make decisions on our behalf, and we may even jump to conclusions. We think in extremes: Things are either all black or all white, and they are either perfect or worthless. There is also an unforgiving mindset that forgives the self. For example, we are too hard on ourselves when we feel lonely or rejected. At the same time, we may misread situations and generalize people around us and their dislike toward us.

How to Counter These Traits

Focusing on flaws will not help, but acceptance will. We need to accept that certain things are not in our hands. We can try believing that being socially awkward, inexperienced, and shy are not negative traits. Every mistake that we make is not a horrible one, and looking for perfect examples in people around us will generally lead us to results in vain. Then, what can we do to improve our situation?

First of all, we need to understand that all humans are not balanced. We are all mixes of different traits, negative and positive, and we need to focus on the traits that work for us. This means you don't have to change your personality 180 degrees to get rid of your shyness, be happier, or attract more friends. You just need to boost your confidence and match your skills with your competing needs to get the desired results. Overexpectations—or underestimations—and a lack of knowledge when it comes to conversation skills can make people introverted, lonely, selective when choosing a company, and inflexible. One way to counter this is to accept that no social behavior is perfect and no one is socially perfect. You may look good, yet change your clothes thrice because how you look affects you. But to those to whom you truly matter, such things will not matter at all. Sometimes we need to weigh the pros and cons of a situation. We need to see how our effort can benefit us. Socializing is challenging, but not socializing is a compromise as well. We should acknowledge that anxiety, awkwardness, and embarrassment can come up at any time, and the best we can do is to accept them as natural parts of ourselves and just be.

Partial or complete avoidance of social situations or bailing out early from events is not the answer. Avoiding a situation may strengthen the fear of such events. Even if you do that at parties, you cannot do that at the office. Work is an everyday social situation and as much as you may dread going to work, you cannot avoid it, and neither can you bail out early. Avoiding social interactions can also push you into isolation, meaning more ways than one to miss out on important opportunities, updates, and connections. The best way to tackle this is by striking up a conversation with anyone around you, even if it's simply asking for a pen. Overt precautions hold us back, but, sometimes, we need to take our chances. It may seem difficult at first, though asking a few simple questions can ease all the tension:

- "Which is your favorite restaurant in the city?"
- "Isn't the weather beautiful today?"

- "I was stuck in a bad traffic jam today. I thought I wouldn't make it to class in time."
- "How are you?"
- "I like your dress. You look very pretty."
- "Want to grab some coffee after work?"

There are ways to distract yourself from your social discomfort, anxieties, insecurities, shyness, and negativity. You can do this by turning them into something positive. Overthinking cannot be helped in certain situations but it is normal to overthink. Do not stop just because your brain wants you to believe, *Oh, I totally ruined my image with that one sentence, I am sure they think I am annoying*, or, *I must be boring because they look disinterested*. Training your mind is about changing your perspective. The more negative and insecure your thoughts are, the more stuck your sentences will be.

Accepting that your palms could be sweaty won't worsen your problem; it prepares you for a challenge. Sometimes acceptance gives us power as opposed to the belief that accepting fears makes us weak, incompetent, and excited. With acceptance, you choose to improve and eliminate the what-ifs. Yes, not all outcomes would be as you anticipated, but it is better to project your energy on an outer result with the potential for improvement rather than shifting it onto internal flaws only you see. Your aim should be to become more social than trying to fit in the mold of acceptance. When you know you are not perfect—and so isn't anyone else—you enjoy being yourself, which is functionally central to realizing that there is nothing wrong with you. We all get jitters of self-doubt. The important thing is to acknowledge the goals that you are after, and at what cost. Maybe hiking in a group is not your thing, but going on a solo hike is. Trying it once will cause no harm. You never know, you may end up picking a new skill or two along the way.

You are not going to live a happier life if you start caring less. Acceptance is the first step toward making positive little changes or proactive measures on this journey. Being shy is not the worst thing ever, so treat yourself as you would treat a friend. Before finding friends in the outer world, our job is to befriend ourselves. Being kind and understanding towards our feelings and insecurities can keep you away from generalization.

Next, acknowledgment makes you comfortable—not too comfortable—with your anxiety. Your anxiety is nothing but a reminder that you care for yourself. Care for yourself so much that you are going to cancel plans to stay at home and "preserve" yourself. In reality, you know that you do not need this kind of preservation. We all need some me time but we need to have some "we time"—that is, social time—to remain human. We are not robots programmed to live in isolation. This could be also one of the causes of our rage. We get extremely frustrated and angry when alone because it hurts to see other people moving on with their lives and friends. Without a social life, we are basically stuck in a world that loses its sense of time and space. For example, being locked in your room can give you the peace you want. You can water your plants every day, play with your pet, and even read books in the quiet of your room, but it isn't the same as going out, meeting people, and learning from your environment. At least you would be happy that you tried and did not let anxiety come your way and run your life. This proactive approach can subvert anxiety, insecurities, and anger. There is nothing more frustrating than being angry and unable to express it. Deep inside, there is a willingness to tell others what is keeping you dissatisfied. It could be because of the way others around you work, past betrayals you have faced, your own trust issues, or the confusion and struggles you face on a daily basis. Being honest about how you feel helps you to express it better. These problems are common but affect people differently. You can try the following:

- **Take slow and deep breaths**: Close your eyes, relax your body, and breathe slowly and deeply. Inhale through your nose and hold your breath for a few seconds to exhale from your mouth. This manipulation of breathing patterns is the quickest way to connect to the self and feel calm. Short and shallow breaths are harsh reminders of being nervous and impatient. On the contrary, regulating breathing helps us to breathe consciously, which we forget so often.

- **Count backward**: People who are not friendly are often perceived as rude. When we say something out of place or on impulse, we trigger this notion further. Ours could be an unintended reaction, but it could be seen as a mean jibe. This is a great way to check your emotions and calm your mind. It may not work for everyone, but stopping before reacting impulsively gives us a window to think clearly. We can take a break and count backward to momentarily detach ourselves from a negative or stressful situation. This break can give us a third-person perspective.

- **Go on a walk to clear your mind**: Walking, especially when in and around nature, helps us to calm down. It is a great gamma-aminobutyric acid (GABA) booster that reduces stress and anxiety and allows clear and creative thinking. It improves observational skills and cognitive function, both of which play a major role in helping us communicate better.

- **Keep yourself hydrated**: Drinking water addresses dehydration of the body and mind and helps us focus better. It has calming effects on us and also helps us sleep better at night. Dehydration, stress, and depression form a vicious cycle. You can break it by keeping yourself hydrated to calm your nerves and improve your body's rest and digestion response.

- **Read and watch positive content**: We can always argue that anxiety makes us more cautious and protects us from danger, but it also makes us passive. To be more active, we need to take a step forward and not backward. Negative thoughts can play the worst-case scenarios on a loop. Positive coping mechanisms break this loop and help us visualize a life that is not going to be so bad after all. A few failures and rejections are destined in every life. Dwelling on positive thoughts encourages risk-taking behavior and moving outside of our comfort zone. As a student, you could play a more active role in group projects; as a working professional, you could be more proactive to present a paper; as a journalist, you would dare to cover, or, rather, unravel, more intense stories. You learn to enjoy new tasks with a renewed passion when your fears decrease. You do not have to force nervousness out of your system to gain more confidence. That happens at its own natural pace. You will always be nervous before trying something new but stick to the mantra of not being afraid of something new.

- **Visualize positive growth**: This is a beautiful way to diffuse negativity. Visualize your goal. If you aim to be more social, visualize it. Look for ways to connect with people. Be a part of conversations, be it virtual or real. Read on things that can make you more aware and participative. Focus the positive light on your future self, and visualize all the good things that can happen to you. This will yield positive outcomes and performances.

- **Get engaged in some kind of physical activity**: Exercising helps us to shed the weight of all negative emotions. It is a great diversion that not only makes us healthy and keeps us active, but also boosts endorphins to reduce anxiety. Regular exercises can alleviate negative feelings and give a natural boost to determination, discipline, and confidence.

- **Journaling helps**: You are being expressive when writing down your thoughts. Expression is a great way to let go of negative things; you detach yourself from feelings of nervousness and anxiety by writing down positive thoughts. We can always forget the negative thoughts once written, but we can always come back to the positive thoughts whenever life seems challenging. Expressing feelings also helps in understanding ourselves better. It gives us a chance to read a particular situation and act accordingly. People who are more expressive find it easier to talk to others, given they are more eloquent with a sharper presence of mind. For example, if you have to go to an official event, you can note down how you are feeling. What is it that makes you nervous? Meeting new people? The food? When you would write these down, you would see your fears are not that irrational, and you will face them in a better manner.

- **Try not to dwell on a negative situation**: The present is quickly over, the past is gone, and the future is yet to come. Dwelling on something that is no longer present or worrying about something that is not yet real ruins what you have in the present. We do that often when nervous, so much so that it becomes a part of our personality.

- **Give yourself a pep talk to move on**: Tell yourself that you are ready for certain things, and, if not, then ask yourself why. It is crucial to think logically when having internal conversations. Emotional conversations with yourself go nowhere; they only confuse you more. When we talk to ourselves, we gain clarity. We are closest to ourselves, so the words we say to ourselves matter a lot. Therefore, use phrases that can help you: "I have got this," "This looks easy," "I can do this," "I am strong," "I am bright," and, "I am deserving." One day, you will thank yourself for this.

- **Choose an activity to relax**: It could be listening to or playing music, gardening, cooking, watching a film, photography, or just sleeping some more hours. Whatever helps us feel fresh and relaxed helps us to clear our thought process and think logically. When we are tired and frustrated, we often think emotionally.

- **Organize your schedule**: We tend to get more nervous when things happen beyond our control. While control is not always a positive activity, having a schedule can help us be more prepared for upcoming meetings, events, or outings. Last-minute preparations can often lead to us forgetting things.

Countering anxiety, fears, nervousness, and insecurities is crucial to developing social skills. Once we are confident enough to engage with other people, these skills develop with practice. The more we meet people, the more socially confident we become. Some people have no problem with social skills, but that is true as long as they are around people they are comfortable with. This is because such people amplify each other's social needs and the interactions are fulfilling and supportive. In an alien setting, with strangers, some people freeze, not because they lack social confidence but because they crave warmth. Such a person may feel that, despite their continuous efforts, the response they receive is not friendly. It's possible to be stuck in such unfriendly situations as well.

How to Make Friends in an Unfriendly Situation

Some situations are tougher than others. Finding friends in places where people are unapproachable can be daunting. In such a situation, the safest step to socialize is to look for someone similar. It is wrong to say that we should not be scared or intimidated in such a situation, but to think that we are the only ones feeling awkward in this social setup is also completely false. For example, if you arrive at a dinner party you had been invited to, and you find people in groups, chatting and enjoying themselves, you may not know how to approach them. The trick here is to find a person who looks approachable and can be bonded with. This can also happen in a new office where people are already divided into cliques, and you have no clue which one to join. Since you are new, you might want to stay away from office politics. The best option in places where you may feel like an outsider is to find a fellow outsider. This is the best approachable choice. This person could be someone like you— new, clueless, nervous, excited, and lonely. However, just because someone is at a table alone having a bite does not mean they are looking for company. You need to first observe the crowd and read their reactions. If someone smiles back, they might be interested in initiating a conversation and perhaps look relieved when you approach them because you saved them from a dreadful boring evening or isolation at the office. A lot of times, welcoming, interesting, bright people suffer because they have no clue how to approach others or be approachable. They are in the same spot as you were, but because you have now improved your skills and are courageous enough to take a chance at making a new friend, you are befriending them as well as helping them.

From the Author's Life

In my personal experience, I have realized no two friendships can ever be close. I know two friendships cannot be the same or equal, but here I want to emphasize that they cannot even be close. The bond we share with every person is unique because they come with their baggage of grief, insecurities, problems, and anxieties, and you come with yours. You two have a profound bond because there is solace in each other's company, and then there is liberation through joy.

Moving to a different country made me value what I had. I always valued the people I had in my life, but now I knew the real reasons why they mattered. The friendships I shared in my home country could not be replicated or replaced. In my new home country, my life was challenged to find friendships that could make me feel the same as my long-standing "best friends" did back home. No matter where you are, you feel the need for your old friends because they are so fulfilling. They complete the circle of your life.

On one of my evening walks, I met two women, and we started talking. I remember them saying, "We are best friends, and we want our kids to be best friends, too." I asked why they felt that was necessary, and the women said that it was because it would deepen their bond of friendship and there would be nothing more joyous to see their kids grow up together. One of the women had a little cute cherub in her arms, while the other was four months pregnant. My heart was full seeing this purity. We can never replace friends. We can add more to our circles and we may feel left behind when some of them move ahead and get by, but few of us are lucky to have them at all.

While I miss my friends from back home, I am extremely fortunate that my circle of friends in my new home gave me the support and love I needed. My friendships here cannot replace or match long-standing bonds but are still extremely fulfilling and sustaining. I can proudly say I was lucky to experience the best of both worlds, but finding friends was not at all easy. It takes time. The fact that I was in a new country meant I had to approach people differently. Not everyone I approached is my friend to this day. I had to learn the polite way my new culture expected me to approach others, and it was definitely different from how we bonded back home. Nevertheless, the meaning and essence of friendships never change. The purity that the heart carries and the genuineness that true friends show when they care for you are universal. It took me a long time to figure that one out and I am happy with where I am today. While I understand the aspect and dynamics of friendship better with experience and time, directly approaching people is still outside my comfort zone. I guess some things never change, and sometimes it's for the better. And so shouldn't we? Because, sooner or later, we do find our tribe when it is meant to be.

Food for Thought

You feel your friend is spectacular but you find it difficult to compliment them. You see them achieving greater heights in their career, and while you are happy for them, your own struggle makes you sad and a bit jealous, too. How can you deal with these petty emotions and move on and be happy for your friend?

An option to consider:

This is not your friend's fault. Their success is an achievement and your underachievement should make neither of you feel small. We all have different lives. Your friend may have made minor but very important life decisions with hard work and discipline that have made them more successful than you. Even if they didn't have to work hard and you feel they were just born lucky or rich, their life is still different from yours. At this point, you can probably consider what they add to your life. Does their presence make you happy? Do they inspire you? In what ways have they helped you? What made you choose them as a friend? And finally, do you want to end this friendship right now? If yes, what will be the consequences?

Chapter 6:
Building a Fulfilling Social Life

We grow up watching films and shows where there are tight-knit groups of friends, and we dream of such friendships during school and college life and beyond. But does any of it last? Not forever. Once we are out of college, everyone goes their separate ways. Friendships, also, do not always turn out the way we wish they did. A lot of times, finding a friend online is more amusing than nostalgic. *Wait, Chris works at a bank now? Gemma has two daughters? Mr. Walter still teaches at the same school?* And then there were friends who always stood by us no matter what. They were our biggest cheerleaders, our biggest supporters, always kind and empathetic to tell us how incredible they felt to have us as their friend. Yes, you are right, the ones we never valued. The friends who we always overlooked. The friends who we dumped to join the more popular group. We all have made certain mistakes in choosing the right friends, haven't we? Even now, many of us run away from colleagues who are too sweet. Maybe we think they're loners and looking for a connection, and we do not want to be their sole connection. Maybe it's because we feel they are uncool and their company would make us look uncool as well, or perhaps we genuinely do not like them. But friendships do blossom in unexpected ways and first impressions are not always the right ones either.

There are so many stories about friends and friendships that can keep us engaged forever. There could have been instances when your life was full of friends who you referred to as your "people," but, today, you know the drift that took everyone away was life's way of telling you that you're on your own. Does this mean you need to stop worrying about friends and start living a life in complete isolation? No close bonds? Everything in vain? At any point in life, we look for people who we can depend on. These become your "people" in that instance. It can get tough when other things take priority. But having some light in your life must also be your priority, and friends bring this light.

The Chosen Family

The thing about the family you choose is that you do not get much of a choice. It is something that happens naturally. You do not step out of your house thinking I will make a friend at the park today. A chosen family is not one with multiple members where if you do not speak to one, you have the option to choose another. A chosen family is where people are involved enough to be there for each other, making unshakeable bonds. It is a family where fights occur but patching up occurs more easily. A chosen family is one that is ready to repair the cracks in the walls of their home. Most conversations for most people occur via text these days. This is unfortunate, because friendships do not sustain via text. You will always wonder what the next person is up to. Chances are that when they go out, they meet more interesting people. You are right about all your insecurities, but just because you do not step out of your comfort zone does not mean others are not moving ahead in life. In a nutshell, you cannot stop your friends from making new friends.

Unrealistic expectations

One thing we have imbibed from the entertainment world is that friends eat and drink together, yet that's not it. They do all the activities together; they cook together, watch films together, make plans together, live together, party together, meet each other's colleagues and families, and are there for each other at every good and bad stage of life. That is something absolutely not possible in the real world. Because these fictional friends are so stuck with each other, they even know what the other person feels without a hint. They know what your needs are, and they will move mountains to do whatever makes you feel better during upsetting times. They fight with and for you, are always present in your life, and make life not just beautiful but also convenient. In the real world, we are all drowning with bills, inflation, and lives of our own. Yes, friends try their best to be there for each other, but they can disappoint as well as forgive. Friendships are never perfect and never the way we see them on our screens.

Another interesting, charming, and unrealistic expectation is to see friends as noncompetitors. We grow up with friends in the same class, go to college with people who we study with, and work with people who could be vying for the same promotion as us. All that does not mean we can't be friends. Competitors can be friends, and friends can also become competitors. There is nothing unhealthy about it. Regardless of this status quo, friends can help us champion our dreams. In fact, this should be seen as an opportunity, because friends from similar fields of work can actually introduce us to the right people who can coach and guide us if needed.

The perfect blend of similarities and dissimilarities in close friends is another myth that people have. We can never weigh these things. There are so many things that can make people similar and dissimilar from each other. Interestingly, two very similar people may have very different points of view about the same thing and can have multitudes of arguments about who's right. They may also disagree with you when you do not have enough faith in yourself. These are the qualities that make each one of us unique, so any concern about how my friend would end up looking silly is baseless. We either disagree with or stand by them in their perspectives and choices.

We do not always end up in the same city as our best friends. And, even if we do, there are always some lonely moments. In a practical world, we cannot have our friends by our side in every tough moment. If you move to a new place, you will have to make new friends, too. You may be alone when you break up, are a bit unwell, or face problems at work. You will have to manage things by yourself despite having your friend in the same city.

Not All Friends Are Best Friends

Despite the thick skin we grow, we are bound to get hurt, and because we get hurt, we take time to heal. The wounds we get and the healing process change us permanently. This world constantly inflicts wounds on us, and we don't always have others present to support us. It is possible that people who care may be undergoing their transformation, so we have to be our own support. While we change, we cannot expect others to be the same. This is a crucial reason why friendships end. People do not remain the same, and it's not something they can be blamed for. This growth happens through a process of learning, unlearning, and relearning, and we have to accept that while growth adds to one aspect of our life, we lose something in another part of our life. Growing apart, hence, becomes a casual yet painful truth of life.

Television shows never fix this growing-apart phase that friends go through. Friends sort everything out, albeit through minor inconveniences, to move back to speaking terms. The hurt in real life remains. Things do not smooth out so easily, and once a friendship is over, it's never the same with the same person or with anyone else. It stops making sense. We can have another great bond, but it's no longer how we had with someone else. Thus, we internalize the pain. It is hard to accept that, despite numerous tries, the bond cannot be mended. Making a best friend again in life is neither disastrous nor impossible, yet it takes time because, once our feelings are hurt once, we then like to tread carefully. On the basis of the kind of connection you form with your friend, your friendship can be defined in a few ways:

- Some friends are casual. You know them, and they know you, but it never goes beyond that. You both are happy to run into each other, but you would not really call them friends. They are more than acquaintances yet less than friends. Such connections can be useful, but too many casual friends without any real friends can make life utterly boring and lonely. If you have many such "friends," it is the same as having no friends at all.

- Then, come friends who are people with whom you have shared real moments of friendship. You know them, have hung out with them, have had some deep conversations with them, and like them. You like the idea of being part of their community, and you do not mind spending time with them. These are the people you know you can trust if needed. However, here's the catch. They may come forward to help you, or they may find an excuse for themselves; in the latter case, you cannot really complain. How you see them can be very different from how they see you. This is why the term "friend" can be very vague and subjective. You don't talk to them every day, but others have an impression that you two are more than casual friends.

- Then, there are few friends who you trust equally. They may not be each other's friends. They may not even know each other, but you are the common link between all of them. These are the people you trust as your second family. They are available, reliable, and honest. You know you can depend on them. If they cannot be available themselves, they'll make it up to you. Having this group is not about having multiple friends but about having at least one friend when things go wrong. These are the people you can text or call in the middle of the night for advice, suggestions, help, and opinions. The idea of having a group of friends is good for as long as peace prevails. When there are different sides during a fight or disagreement, it's not the most healthy thing for a group of friends. Similarly, not all issues get sorted on a group chat. A group of friends carry the responsibility to stick together. Group friendships can become a big strength but they can also turn into a quick mess if every member isn't kept on the same page. Not all group friendships go this far, because keeping a group together takes a lot of work.

- And, finally, there's your closest friend—your best friend—the one who is always the first to know everything. They are your emergency contact and your biggest supporter. They are the friend-soulmate you always wanted and needed, and this feeling is mutual from both ends. It is common to have more than one best friend, but you can never have more than two best friends. Most people prefer one best friend over many friends, and this is probably the reason behind loneliness and loss when this pure relationship ends. To many people, it feels right to be devoted and loyal to just one person. It is about finding "your one and only" in a circle of friends. But here's the thing: The best-friends-forever (BFF) tag does not work for every individual. People change, as do their interests, circumstances, and personalities. To have a BFF is a lucky thing because the universe does not always magically work in favor of two individuals. People fight, fail to right their wrongs, and say things that they should have not. They also may not forgive and forget for the rest of their lives. There are numerous stories like that. Once this friendship is sabotaged, it is near impossible to have another of the same kind and intensity.

When we add someone to our life, we include them with the belief that they'd pick up our call if we dial their number. These are not random people chosen just because we felt inspired or attracted. These are people who possess certain traits that led us to believe we can trust them, and trust is the biggest currency used when making new friends. We start blaming ourselves when we feel we failed to find one person—forget four or five people—who can understand, support, and truly see us for who we are. It is traumatic, and it can make us feel petty, when we don't have anyone to hold and cry. We blame ourselves for the inability to fix this condition. We feel bad that despite friends being a choice, we do not have the option to make this choice. It often feels unfair that we have not managed to find our "people" yet.

Keep Talking

Sometimes a person could be visibly upset, annoyed, or frustrated. The cause behind this could be related or unrelated to you. To keep talking to them does not mean to keep speaking when they seem least interested. There are inappropriate times when we must try not to unintentionally violate any boundaries. This means we need to find an opportune time to ask the right questions. A person who's silent could be under extreme stress or upset over something that is deeply affecting them. In such cases, asking questions is direct and rude. The most we can do is to tell them that we are around in case they need us.

When saying "call me when you need me," you put the onus on the other person to reach out. This is both good and bad. This gesture is good for friends who are independent and emotionally more mature. With people who have a sensitive dominant side, their approach has to be more careful. The following sentences can be very reassuring for people who are shy and unable to express their pain:

- "I hope you are okay."
- "Is there anything I can do for you?"
- "I hope you know I am there for you."
- "I'm just a call away."
- "Do you want me to stay with you?"
- "I care about you."

To keep talking means to keep continuing to have a connection. People face terrible things in life, but it is their friends who are their immediate help. If you are someone whose friend is facing troubles, you need to make sure that they know you are beside them. You don't have to literally speak with them every day; it is the mere presence that does all the talking.

Food for Thought

You are very particular about punctuality because you greatly value time. You feel it's one thing that should matter a lot, because time equals money and money is essential. However, your best friend is always late, and nothing irritates you more than that. How can you deal with such a situation?

An option to consider:

This is something you should not take personally because we all view time and its value differently. You want to know how much you gained in one hour; your friend, on the other hand, might want to measure the laughs they laughed and focus on having a life well lived in a certain span of time. Your management accuracy should not, however, depend on your friend's mismanagement of time. Do not compromise with your values, but don't eliminate a friend or let this be a cause of friction between you two. For example, if you're leaving work early to meet a friend at 5 p.m., continue working for 30 more minutes more without any hassle. Similarly, if you are meeting them for lunch or dinner, you can always be 15–20 minutes late. I know it's unlike you if you manage time very well, but you are still managing time by investing it somewhere you need it more without compromising your friendship. You are avoiding shouting at your friend and you are avoiding their, as well as your own, embarrassment. But, of course, do not be late if you have to drop them off at the airport in time to catch their flight.

Chapter 7:
Building Trust and Developing Meaningful Connections

It takes work to build trust, just as it takes work to sustain a relationship after we have built trust. Before we establish trust, we need to understand the meaning of trust. It can mean different things to different people, but, one thing is for sure, it cannot be something superficial. If you place your trust in a person, thing, institution, or promise, you believe in the truth they speak. You want to feel they are reliable and that their ability to uphold this truth is strong. Trust lays a strong basis for your relationship with others and yourself. It helps you feel secure and guide you with making important decisions in life.

Why Is Trust Important?

Trust is a brave lesson in itself. When we talk about qualities that virtuous humans must have, trust is one of the fundamentals. We want to surround ourselves with people who we know we can talk to, who would show up for us, listen to us, and value the bond we share. Trust is a priority because it reminds us that it can be a strong factor in binding two or more people to have a meaningful connection. This brave attempt of trusting others comes with certain conditions. When we trust someone, there is an unsaid understanding that the two people involved would respect these conditions. When these conditions are violated, we tend to have trust issues. These are not restrictive or limiting conditions that force you to have a narrow viewpoint. These conditions are personally set, independently followed, and mutually respected. What are these conditions, and why is it so hard to trust someone if they violate these conditions?

Why Is Trusting Others Difficult for Some People?

I would like to trust a person who I know is worth trusting. This is a condition most people have before they tend to trust anyone in life. Of course, there are people who would like us to believe that someone they trust is worth our trust, too. However, trusting someone is a very personal experience. It is not limited to personal affliction. It is a journey in gaining life experience.

If you feel it is difficult for you to trust others, it is possible that your trust was broken in the past. We are what our experiences make us. Trust, as a characteristic, is no different. Our encounter with this characteristic can greatly affect our life and behavior. The reason you may have trust issues is not because you lack trust but rather because you feel trust is central to your existence. It is so important to you that the people who you trust have to be special, as that is a critical part of how you want to relate to others. You know very well that trusting the wrong person may disturb your peace and affect your overall well-being, and because of its significance in a healthy and long-lasting relationship, you want to make sure you are not hurt trusting the wrong person.

Trust issues can manifest in the wildest of ways. But another unimaginable reality is how we like to keep our guards up to protect ourselves when we're vulnerable. In difficult moments, we resist risking our feelings being hurt any further, but our minds keep questioning the other person and our trust in them. It is harmful because it can

- breed irresponsibility and misunderstandings.
- disrupt peace.
- keep us anxious and depressed.
- make us assume the worst.
- trigger bad memories.
- ruin good moments.
- trigger loneliness and isolation.
- replace forgiveness and love with bitterness and ungratefulness.
- harbor unwillingness to commit.
- sabotage the lives involved.

These trust issues can take a toll on our physical, mental, and emotional health. Navigating interpersonal connections may pose a challenge to you because you cannot trust when you want to trust. When your mind is torn between two opposites, it decides to hold itself back when wanting to give in. What does this mean? It means that you want to rely on someone and trust them, but you also fear vulnerability. To get close to another person, we have to reveal ourselves.

We base our trust on the social interaction we might have had with the person, the culture that influences them, the company they choose, and the experiences they have had. Our trust is also based on other people's opinions of us. If we get safe vibes, we feel the person is worth trusting. We will see ahead in this chapter why this quality matters when trying to build friendships by winning the trust of the other person.

Trust is not born in one day. Trust is earned. It is important to open up when you are ready to open up. At the same time, it is pertinent to consider the causes behind why you've built walls around yourself. The process of trusting others begins with trusting ourselves and our strengths.

Trusting Yourself Before Trusting Others

Before we move on to see how trust works between two people, we need to understand the value of trust in oneself. Just as trust brings two people closer, trusting ourselves can bring us closer to our own being. People are hardwired to connect with other people around them. To enable this connection, humans have to look deeper into the world that's within them. They have to connect with and understand themselves. If you can place trust in yourself, you reassure yourself that you are strong, are confident, and can look for possible solutions to the problems you'll face in the future. We do not want others to criticize us, yet we are our own worst critics. Being too hard on oneself is possible in the case of people with trust issues. They want to portray a perfect image. They want to look strong, independent, and busy, but they fail to look believable. To trust ourselves more, we have to learn to

- be more vulnerable.
- be less self-critical.
- face our fears.
- identify our experiences with names.

- be our own cheerleader.
- appreciate the good in life.

The Power of Vulnerability in Building Trust

Vulnerability gives the other person a chance to understand your needs and desires better. It makes the bond between two people stronger and more satisfying. Vulnerability is also a sign of strength and not weakness. We may like our privacy a lot more than vulnerability. We would like to consider the effect of sharing sensitive and personal details with others, and rightly so. But confiding in someone you consider close is a step-by-step process.

The best part about being vulnerable is that you are being your authentic self. There is no copying, there is no hiding. There are weaknesses that reveal courage, and in that courage is a promise that you are not afraid to show your wounds. Vulnerability is a love letter to your pain and trauma and an invitation to those who trust to come and witness your story of power. Vulnerability is powerful because your truth becomes the only armor that you hold to protect yourself.

Vulnerability does not give you a show-cause notice like your fears do. It is not adamant on changing your perception, rather it allows you to reimagine life and ways of living. When you show vulnerability, you tell the other person that they can keep their guard down, too. You tell them that you trust them and that you can be trusted back. In a way, you are taking your share of the responsibility to own your emotions—which may sometimes even cause a mess. Vulnerability is a healthy outlet for emotions. Repressed emotions are the feelings we unconsciously avoid. Vulnerability is a way to consciously face them, because feelings cannot be put into a box. They should not be aggressively encountered, but they can also not be ignored just because facing them is uncomfortable.

Once we learn to face them and be vulnerable, we build trust through meaningful connections. It is this connection that keeps us alive. It gives meaning and purpose to life. Connection is not about superficial conversations or belonging to a community; it is something deeply felt and at an individual level. More importantly, people who do not feel connected will understand the value of connection better because they know what exclusion feels like.

Vulnerability is an important aspect of connection because it supersedes a person's ability to connect over any kind of guilt or shame they may have about their self-image or personal problems. Shedding this shame is important for gaining confidence. Confident people have a sense of belonging and feel loved and appreciated. On the contrary, people who are not confident will feel a lack of belonging. They do not know if they are good enough. While the former can successfully communicate because they know their vulnerability and feelings will not be judged, the latter feel they don't deserve love or attention. Their struggle to feel belonged is the real contributor to their feelings of exclusion. The shift from feeling like an outsider to one who belongs is a long journey, and this change is not possible without understanding the value of vulnerability.

Learning the Vulnerability Values

Vulnerability is the key ingredient in your recipe for human connection. Your courage to be vulnerable and your compassion for other people's vulnerability are the supporting ingredients this recipe requires. As you embrace who you are, you connect to your real self. With this courage, you can approach another person who is brave enough to be their true self. Hence, when we embrace vulnerability, we open our hearts to newer possibilities in our effort to build relationships. We have warmth and acceptance in our hearts. While there is fear of rejection, there is no fear of expression. You celebrate your achievements just as you celebrate your defeats. You are ready to talk about them, to share your experiences. In short, you are open to celebrating your existence.

When we are vulnerable, we are complete. We refuse to live life in pieces, though we tend to value the broken pieces more. Being vulnerable can be painful yet comforting and rewarding. Being vulnerable is not just about sharing the darker secrets of life; it is also about expressing your love first. In a world where people want to keep their pieces together, vulnerability makes us more human. You can be vulnerable in your physical, emotional, or mental state—or all three. You may want to randomly begin sharing your thoughts, have an unexpected urge to cry, or feel an unusual need for a hug. Although we feel that these vulnerable moments can make us look weak, this will not bother you after a certain point. After all, who does not want to earn a true friend in exchange. It is not that dangerous a gamble, is it?

Cultivating Empathy

Another quality that makes us more human and approachable is empathy. Empathy is cultivated with experience and kindness. A heart full of empathy will not overlook the pain to view the joy. A greater part of empathy is about acknowledging the pain and how much it hurts. It is the ability to understand the sorrow of the other person. It is also the willingness to share their feelings, especially pain. When you empathize with someone, you listen to them. By making them feel heard, you give them a safe space to just be themselves. In short, you let them be vulnerable.

Empathizing means being curious about a person's ordeals without being intrusive. It is listening to them with patience and intent. There is an element of kindness accompanying your behavior. Imagine a scenario where a newcomer joins your department. She is an immigrant who's probably just trying to find her way through things. Now, she is shy because she's new, but she probably also feels out of place because of cultural differences. Others, too, are not too keen to readily interact with her because she seems reserved. Say that, one day, you are about to join your friends during the lunch break like the rest of the days, but you overhear her speaking over the phone. She seems so tense that you even notice her voice cracking. You do not know how to approach her or if it is the right thing to do at all, but you finally gain enough courage and walk up to her to ask, "Is everything all right?" Not only does she share everything, but she also thanks you for listening to her. Your behavior now determines how empathetic you are:

- Do you invite this new person to the table with the rest of the group?
- Do you leave them like that?
- Do you walk back to your table and discuss what just happened?

- Do you say nothing and continue your lunch as if nothing happened?
- Do you feel sorry for them for the rest of your day?
- Do you feel you wasted your time?

Empathy is different from sympathy, because while there is an understanding of the other person's distress or loss, there is no pity or feeling sorry. When there is empathy, there's an effort and ability to understand the other person's problems, not a relief that you aren't going through the same. This makes empathy a more intense emotion as there are genuine feelings involved; you try to imagine the scale of pain as you imagine or witness the circumstances. Sometimes you even sense the other person's anguish without them sharing or expressing anything. Heightened awareness and sensitivity can make you more empathetic. With empathy, you can build a natural and emotional connection through cognition with other individuals. When you show empathy, you

- focus on similarities and not the differences.
- imagine yourself in another person's shoes.
- look for a genuine connection and not superficial conversations.
- look at the world beyond yourself.

In effect, empathy can make people kinder. It is the opposite of narcissism. Just because you are ready to open up and share your experiences does not mean that you're looking for validation. It is a genuine connection that you seek. Empathetic people may make friends more easily because of how they can relate to other people. Additionally, the relationships they form may be more meaningful.

While empathy comes more naturally to some people, it is practiced over time. You do not want kindness to take you over and drain you of energy. An empathetic person does not just respond. They go a step further and try to gain a new perspective to understand the other person's emotions and hardships. The other kind of empathy is when you intellectually perceive behaviors and emotions through situations and experiences.

This cognitive skill is practiced and learned with time. While intuitive empathy is emotional, cultivated empathy is cognitive.

From Feeling Empathetic to Making Friends

This journey becomes fairly simple when we see ourselves in other people. Empathetic people can also show their sensibility toward other causes, such as animals, the environment, and the poor and hungry. A lot of times, these initiatives can bring similar people together who work for the same causes, attend meetings and rallies, and even form close-knit groups of friends. Because of their power to resonate with others and their ability to care for others, they understand why it is necessary to coexist without having to agree with everything that the other offers. This is a great way to avoid conflict because there is comprehensive learning, recognizing, reasoning, sharing, and accommodation of feelings.

Active Participation

Active participation is all about making efforts, big and small, to build trust and to sustain a relationship. Let us look at a few ways through which we can develop trust in friendships:

- **Be honest.** No matter what the cost, always tell the truth. Be the person your friend needs and can trust, not someone who is a false mirror.
- **Be considerate.** You can be kind even while being truthful no matter how harsh the truth is.
- **Make time for your friends.** Trust comes with communication, and communication comes with time.
- **Be reliable.** We all want to have friends who are dependable. Learn to keep secrets.
- **Value your friend's time and emotions.**
- **Do not believe in rumors.** Avoid spreading them, too.
- **Listen without bias.** Try not to intervene, and listen wholeheartedly without giving suggestions or advice.

- **Encourage your friend to follow their dream.** Compassion, courage, loyalty, and concern play a great role in supporting your friend and reminding them of their skills and strengths.

- **Be secure in your mind and emotions.** Do not try to be that friend who is always worried, possessive, or insecurely attached to friends.

From the Author's Life

You do not always need common interests to form meaningful friendships. For me, a meaningful friendship must have several components. I know, especially in today's world, demanding a lot is unfair. We already walk under a lot of pressure in life, and if that weren't enough, expectations tend to hurt us, too. This is why most of us do not keep many expectations, nor do we give false impressions. However, friendship is one arena where genuine expectations are the norm. This is because we make friends to have a balanced life.

Because so many of us are so genuinely committed and honest, we are scared to invest in new relations for fear of being disappointed. We are scared that our love and values won't be reciprocated by an equal measure, yet relationships cannot be built on these expectations. We have to put in the effort and open up to help the other person see the real us. This is the first step toward being vulnerable. Vulnerability is closely tied to trust. When we are sure we can trust them, we exchange our fears with a willingness to trust them. It is a beautiful feeling to finally let go of fears and share our thoughts and secrets. This is also a sign of reliability.

My best friend and I are polar opposites, but we trusted each other and WE were strong enough to be vulnerable with each other. This is the kind of strength we need when we wish to form everlasting friendships.

Food for Thought

Birthdays and anniversaries are personally significant to all of us. Let's say it is your friend's first wedding anniversary. You want to buy something special for them, but it's the end of the month and you are a little strapped for cash. How will you gift your friend on this special occasion?

An option to consider:

Just be honest. There is no shame here. You have a close friend whom you want to give something special to, so you don't have to be sorry if you deliver on that promise even if it is a little late. In most cases, we try to save money but emergencies can come up anytime. If you feel you are in a situation where you want to give something nice to your friend but lack the necessary funds at the moment, you can also tell them that their gift has not arrived yet or that they will have to wait for their gift for a few more days. There comes a point when friendships are way beyond exchange of gifts. Yes, giving is special, but so is honesty and sincerity. There are some things your friend would always be understanding about without you making them cover every detail.

Chapter 8:
Are You Alone or Lonely?

Being alone is the state of being; that is, it is a physical state. Being lonely is a state of mind; it is a feeling. We can be alone and still not feel lonely. On the other hand, we may be surrounded by people and still feel lonely. Loneliness is also different from solitude. No one wants to feel lonely, while many others enjoy solitude. Loneliness is an undesired feeling as it can make a person feel empty, dejected, unwanted, and isolated. People who enjoy solitude like their own company. Lonely people crave human connection. It is important to note that loneliness is both a feeling and a barrier. A lonely person may want to connect with others but still find it impossible to do that. This is because social isolation can cause other health conditions like anxiety and depression. It can make people nervous and dim their confidence. It persists as an overbearing isolation, while solitude is a choice that people make. In isolation, lonely people are not at peace. Loneliness can be of four types:

- social
- emotional
- situational
- chronic

Solitude and the Sense of Contentment With the Self

The words "solitude" and "loneliness" cannot be used interchangeably just because they both refer to the state of being alone. People prefer solitude because of the comfort it provides them. They choose it because it is pleasant and peaceful to them. These people are neither lonely nor unhappy or depressed due to not having friends, but, rather, they choose to not have company because they feel self-sufficient. Their positive state of mind gives them the balance to support themselves. Therefore, it is a misconception that a person who loves solitude is antisocial. A person who can survive alone may also have many friends. Their state of mind is not isolated even if their physical state is. On the other hand, a lonely person has a negative state of mind that can affect their health as well. Their loneliness persists even when they're in the company of others.

The state of solitude makes some people happy and content, meaning they are at peace in their own company. They may engage in activities like binge-watching their favorite shows, reading books they like, going for walks, cooking alone, or meditating. People who have a family may also prefer solitude on days when they want to recharge their batteries and feel rejuvenated. They prefer alone time because this is the commitment they make to themselves: to take good care of themselves, have some alone time, create some personal space, and have others respect their boundaries.

How Does Solitude Add to Having Better Relationships or Maintaining Good Friendships?

Relationships require heavy emotional investment. You have to nourish them with time and energy. It can drain you sometimes, especially when you have to put in extra effort. On some other days, your input has to be greater than the other person's. It is natural to desire some alone time in such situations to preserve your emotional stamina and stability and also preserve your sanity. Solitude can help you grow as a person because it gives you much-needed freedom in straining situations. It's something that you choose, not something that you are forced to follow. When you give yourself some time to understand what you truly desire, it helps you get better acquainted with yourself. And here lies the key to maintaining good friendships and relationships in life. When a person knows themselves well, it is easier for them to know others well. With emotional stability and independence, we are better equipped to handle relationships. We understand how much work it takes to hold people together and in which direction, and we soon find ourselves working in that direction patiently. When we're clueless about what we want from a certain friendship, we tend to blame the other person. We are confused and frustrated because our efforts do not seem to be bearing any desired results. Overworked people often feel overcommitted and underappreciated. They overextend their warmth and gratitude often to find themselves deeply disconnected. Their love is not always equally reciprocated.

Solitude provides a much-needed respite from this daily turmoil. It allows us to explore ourselves. We can sit back, relax, and assess what we bring to relationships as opposed to what the other person does. This single preference we give to ourselves can be misunderstood. If you are someone who is suddenly less interactive and more isolated, people can even go on to say that you have changed or are arrogant. But this self-preservation method has its own benefits. Solitude helps a person

- understand their interests better.
- cultivate new interests and develop their personality.
- learn something new by investing more time in themselves.
- be less anxious.
- feel more independent.
- get more creative with more time that they now have in hand.
- have more productive thoughts.
- explore their purpose beyond petty beliefs.

Solitude is crucial in a busy world. One deserves a well-meaning break to connect to their thoughts, needs, desires, and feelings on a deeper level. How we connect with ourselves plays a special role in determining how we connect with others. This is because solitude maintains a balance in adult life. We are not just passively present in a relationship; we actively evolve with it. Any collaboration or positive engagement is modeled on how well meaning it is for us and the other person. The well-meaning component of life is complemented by a balance of human interaction and solitude. We live and act in solitary roles just as we live and act in communal roles. The solitude we experience enhances the quality of the relationships we are in. If you are in a well-meaning relationship, all your friends and relatives will understand your deep desire to remain solitary at times. They likely also know how it is more like a basic need to preserve yourself rather than a basic desire.

A global pandemic is an example of this. While it disconnected us from all our loved ones, we had their immediate and constant support through the virtual world. At the same time, this disconnection gave us an opportunity to stop the mindless scrolling, set our mobile phones aside, and just breathe. We were forced to look around, water our plants, keep our surroundings clean, arrange our closets, and declutter our lives. In this forced activity, many found solace. A lot of us did not even know how we missed peace in our lives. On the other end of this extreme, people also faced anxiety and grave panic when they found themselves lonely during the pandemic. In effect, forced isolation can be very impatience- and fear-inducing. With few or no people to stay in touch with, loneliness can be burdensome. Solitude is not just for leisure. Yes, people choose it for enjoyment and relaxation, but it can help people generate empathy and regulate extreme emotions.

From the Author's Life

It took us many years for my best friend and I to get to where we are—from colleagues to best friends—but, today, we stand at a point where attempts to make each other feel special are effortless.

The strength that supported our friendship was the value of loyalty. We both are brutally loyal to each other, and that has helped us survive over the years. We know we respect each other and protect each other. We both have stood beside each other in the most difficult times and have never thrown each other under the bus. We never make each other feel vulnerable or awkward in front of others, and that is a huge assurance.

A splash of fun and laughter never hurts, too. It is a medicine that always works. Life would be colorless without people who you can have fun with. While these relations are about common interests, habits, and hobbies to some extent to meet the right friends, don't be disappointed if you meet someone who is not like you. Try to step out of your comfort zone and let the experience absorb you just as you absorb the experience. Never forget that the other person may have the same fears and apprehensions as you, and you can be their support as they can be yours. What else is friendship?

Food for Thought

Your friend has had a tough childhood. On some nights, they get terrible dreams. There have been times when they have called you when they felt sick due to these nightmares. Tomorrow you have to wake up early for a meeting, but your friend has called you at 1 a.m. What is your reaction, and how do you intend to balance this situation?

An option to consider:

If you have a friend who is emotionally dependent on you—that too at a very vulnerable point in their life—it is your duty to be by their side. Taking a call when you have a meeting next is difficult, but you can convince yourself to do it for a person who matters to you. For the sake of all the times you were dependent on them, you need to be there for them, too. Just as our work is a part of us, the relationships we have and the bonds we build have an equally important part to play in our lives. This also means we have to consider how our work keeps us going, and so do our friends, who are our support system. Jobs come and go, but friends live forever. You cannot, and should not, ignore your work for anything. And if you are a tad bit afraid that this can become a routine, you can gently remind your friend—at a later instance, obviously—that you took their call when you had a meeting the next morning. Try not to be arrogant, harsh, or insensitive when you do this. You have no obligation to take their call, because you chose to attend their call. A true friend understands the boundaries, but a true friend also tries their best to support another friend.

Conclusion:
Continuing the Journey

Being friends with someone new is taking a chance, and no one likes to take chances. However, not being friends with anyone is a series of missed opportunities. How do we then know when to act? How do we trust someone? Above all, how do we trust ourselves before making such a decision?

The Leap of Faith

We strive to establish trust in every relationship we build. This faith is a testament to the power we show in ourselves and the belief in our values. We want to believe that we are trusting the right people and that we are capable enough to take such a risk. For some people, just before they take this step, they experience panic, reluctance, and fear, which is most common among people who are the most committed. But here is the twist: Taking this leap of faith can empower, not endanger, you. We need to take this risk to make mistakes, learn from them, evolve, and be more human. After all, trusting another human is a beautiful humane act that is complete in itself. This is because it completes and compensates us physically, mentally, and emotionally. It also compliments our judgment and regardless of the consequences, this leap of faith makes us better people and motivates us to grow beyond mediocrity when it comes to relationships. It gives us a chance to be more excited, thankful, embracing, and brave. Being in touch with other people helps us understand their perspective on things, and that can never hurt. It makes us more hopeful; there is no flaw in that.

Optimizing Your Potential

Connecting with yourself is often like looking for a misplaced thing that you know matters a lot to you without realizing how much it affects you. It's not in everyone's nature to connect to themselves, but the key to connecting with yourself is observation.

Observing your feelings, recognizing them, naming them, and then identifying them with those names is one of the best ways to become familiar with yourself. Another observation one needs to make is how much they invest in self-care. Self-care is not self-indulgence. It is not buying expensive things for yourself. It is not always about going on vacations. You can pay much attention to yourself even in the comforts of your home. This is one thing that people in relationships tend to forget, too.

How much money you spend on family vacations or how expensive your gifts are for your friends and loved ones may seem important. However, how much time you spend with them and the memories you create is equally important. Life always comes back to the moments of laughter and grief that were shared together. When it comes to self-care, too, the priority has to be on how you take care of yourself rather than on how much you spend on yourself. It is about investing in little things that make you happy.

Self-care is also about disconnecting from the virtual world. The number of likes and comments on a photo can indeed make you happy, but think about a world that is connected only via these comments and likes. Imagine how gloomy a world of that sort would be if there is no expression of love, no warm hugs, no genuine concern, and no hot meals to share. Similarly, the food of the soul comes from activities that warm your heart, not from technology. It could be knitting, hiking, reading, meditation, or just taking your pet on a walk. Anything that interrupts your presence with yourself needs to be interrupted. It could be the technology, the people around you, your responsibilities, your daily chores, and even your routine. No matter what, you have to accept that you owe some time to yourself; this acceptance only improves your life and your connection to your surroundings. Everything you need to improve your relationships with others trails back to you and your potential to make meaningful changes, both big and small.

Reflections on the Journey of Making Friends

Socialization is a type of networking that is goal oriented. For example, if you need something to be done but don't know a particular person, you would try to see how you could reach them. Perhaps someone you know may know them or may have worked with them before. This networking helps you gain information about the person, their working style, and reputation. Networking can help one build new connections or get a job, service, product, and fair feedback. Sometimes being with people helps us be more present. It makes interactions more interesting and realistic. Having credible social skills can

- make you happy and cared for.
- make you feel included in new settings.
- make others around you feel included.
- help you gain a perspective beyond yourself.
- ward off depression, aloofness, and loneliness.
- instill confidence in you.
- have a bunch of people you can rely on and share your feelings and thoughts with.
- make you feel healthy and like you belong.

The church community, your golf club friends, your friends at your pet groomer, long lost friends, new friends, colleagues and family members who are friends, friends with who you catch the bus daily, fitness freak friends, friends who are foodies, and any and every friend—all these people have the power to bring joy and light to your life. Similarly, you may not know this today, but your efforts to reach someone and get to know them can change their life as well. Socialization means to be a part of someone's life while letting them be a part of your life. It can boost your confidence and help you have a purpose in life, especially if you are socializing for a cause. It can help you fight stress, loss, grief, and depression, too. In effect, socialization is about spending time with people that you like and about the love for causes you care about. It can make you feel secure by helping you overcome a self-defeating feeling. Some people see socializing as a shallow attempt. They feel making too many friends is akin to having no friends at all. Any relationship is shallow only when it is based on shallow reasons. The quality of your relationship with other people depends on how much you care about each other.

Being Your Best Self While Trying to Make New Friends

Here are some quick tips to recap:

- Recognize your feelings.
- Follow your interests, hobbies, and the skills you want to nurture.
- Never be scared to initiate a conversation.
- Do not socialize with the aim to impress anyone.
- Listen with both your ears and heart.
- Be unafraid about complimenting others.
- Be unapologetically spontaneous.
- Learn to ask the right questions to the right people at the right time.
- Know your limits and maintain healthy boundaries.

Encouraging Yourself to Continue

There could be times when you may feel your efforts and investments aren't reciprocated. You may feel you are ready to listen, but there is no one to listen to you. You may feel uncared for or taken for granted. It is here that you have to remind yourself that being friendly is not about pleasing others. You are an active participant just as you are an active recipient in a relationship. Despite your affection for some people, you have to distance yourself from them if you are unappreciated. You may receive equal or more care and affection from someone else who values you more. Putting yourself out there is not easy, and you must do that only for people who are worth it. Choosing friends is about sharing a pizza as well as sharing each other's burdens. You should

- look forward to spending time with these people.
- not feel your opinions go unheard.
- not feel obliged to fulfill other people's expectations if it makes you uncomfortable.

- be able to know when you are being manipulated or forced to do something.
- listen to your instinct.
- not socialize just because others have told you to do so.

To make new friends, you have to learn the art of small talk. Initiating conversation can be hard for you, but try not to push it lest you look rude. Remember, many people prefer not to respond to a stranger if they do not have a reason or inclination to. Generally speaking, some genius icebreakers may include the following:

- favorite or most popular shows that people binge-watch
- the political, economic, or social state of the world
- food
- travel
- weather
- mental health

Active listening is another way to communicate to the other person that they are being seen and heard. This gives a major boost to their confidence. The interest you show through body language, eye contact, and undivided interest can earn you an admirer instantly. Talking over them or claiming their time and space can make them uncomfortable and impatient. But your natural curiosity to know more about them and ask genuine questions lets you know where they're coming from and lets them know that they're respected.

Lastly, this involvement can be used for more productive interactions. People volunteer for social causes, go to campaign rallies, join animal rescue teams, volunteer for initiatives like food distribution or blind reading, or join a group that grows organic food. This way, people do not limit their interactions, and meeting a diverse range of people also keeps communication exciting. Being part of a service and giving back to society is a great way to feel adequate. There is no misplaced emotion with a misplaced sense of being. You are not dependent on a person to feel valid or valued.

As you aim for quality over quantity, make sure you say a proper goodbye to everyone before entering your sacred space. This space must give you the freedom to be expressive, even in your solitude. Your healing space must be evident enough to tell you that your worth doesn't lie in the quantity of friends you have. Your worth lies in how you see yourself. People who know how to regulate their emotions tend to have a stronger and longer span of stable friendships. You do not have to tag yourself as an "extrovert" to have true friends. Your motivation should emanate from the values you hold. This depends on how comfortable and content you are in life. A person who has many friends may still feel lonely, anxious, and discontent in life. Their attempts to lead several different lives and embody false emotions can drain them of all the energy they have, preventing them from leading any life with simplicity. This whole concept of expanding your horizons and breaking the mold may draw you to newer people and activities, but hold your steps and move forward only when you are ready. After all, this mold that you are born with is precious. To expand your horizon, you may have to expand your experience, but always and necessarily on your own terms.

References

Centers for Disease Control and Prevention. (n.d.). *Loneliness and social isolation linked to serious health conditions*. U.S. Department of Health and Human Services. https://www.cdc.gov/aging/publications/features/lonely-older-adults.html

Cooks-Campbell, A. (2022, May 16). *Pandemic awkwardness holding you back? 10 tips to rediscover your social self*. BetterUp. https://www.betterup.com/blog/how-to-improve-social-skills

Crino, E. (2018, July 20). *6 tips for building trust in yourself*. Healthline. https://www.healthline.com/health/trusting-yourself

Jiang, X. (2018, November 5). *Prefrontal cortex: Role in language communication during social interaction*. IntechOpen. https://www.intechopen.com/chapters/62392

Johns Hopkins Medicine. (n.d.). *Risk factors for heart disease: Don't underestimate stress*. https://www.hopkinsmedicine.org/health/wellness-and-prevention/risk-factors-for-heart-disease-dont-underestimate-stress

Melville, H. (n.d.). *We cannot live only for ourselves. A thousand fibers connect us with our fellow men; and among those fibers, as sympathetic threads, our actions run as causes, and they come back to us as effects* [Quote]. Goodreads. https://www.goodreads.com/quotes/156835-we-cannot-live-only-for-ourselves-a-thousand-fibers-connect

Mental Health First Aid USA. (2019, August 22). *Why healthy friendships are more important for mental health*. National Council for Mental Wellbeing. https://www.mentalhealthfirstaid.org/2019/08/why-healthy-friendships-are-important-for-mental-health/

Miller, H. L. (2023, March 31). *Ambivert vs. omnivert: Which is a better leader?* https://leaders.com/articles/leadership/ambivert-vs-omnivert/

Ng, R. (2021, August 19). *Your kids might now be socially awkward—and they are not alone.* National Geographic. https://www.nationalgeographic.com/family/article/your-kids-might-now-be-socially-awkwardand-theyre-not-alone

Roy, G. (n.d.). *Jung's theory of introvert and extrovert personalities.* Fractal Enlightenment. https://fractalenlightenment.com/31622/life/jungs-theory-of-introvert-and-extrovert-personalities

Santos-Longhurst, A. (2018, July 31). *Can stress make you sick?* Healthline. https://www.healthline.com/health/can-stress-make-you-sick

Sutradhar, D. (2022, October 30). *Socialization—meaning, characteristics, types and nature.* Your Smart Class. https://yoursmartclass.com/socialization-its-meaning-characteristics-types-and-nature/

Wooll, M. (2022, June 1). *Make the connection: 10 effective ways to connect with people.* BetterUp. https://www.betterup.com/blog/how-to-connect-with-people

Printed in Dunstable, United Kingdom

76402402R00057